BUSH TUCKER

Field Guide

Les Hiddins

Explore Australia Publishing Pty Ltd
85 High Street, Prahran, Victoria 3181, Australia

This edition published by Explore Australia Publishing Pty Ltd, 2003

Reprinted 2004

First published by Penguin Books Australia Ltd, 2001

The material in this book originally appeared in *Explore Wild Australia with the Bush Tucker Man*, published by Penguin Books Australia Ltd, 1999

ISBN 1 74117 028 1

10 9 8 7 6 5 4 3 2

Printed in China by Midas Printing (Asia) Ltd

National Library of Australia
Cataloguing-in-Publication data

Hiddins, L. J., 1946–.
Bush tucker field guide.

Includes index.
ISBN 1 74117 028

1. Wild plants, Edible – Australia, Northern – Identification. 2. Wild foods – Australia, Northern – Identification. I. Title.

581.6320994

Publisher's Note

Every effort has been made to ensure that the information in this book is accurate at the time of going to press. The author and the publisher cannot accept responsibility for any errors or omissions. The publisher welcomes information regarding changes and suggestions for future editions. Email: explore@hardiegrant.com.au

Readers are advised that it is their responsibility to ensure that they are not trespassing on Aboriginal land, or contravening laws or regulations by disturbing fauna or flora in national parks or on crown or private land.

WARNING

Certain native and introduced plants can be highly toxic and in some cases consuming them can be fatal. The author and publisher cannot take responsibility for any illness, injury or ailment brought on through consuming or handling plants. It is not recommended that readers use plants for medicinal purposes.

Contents

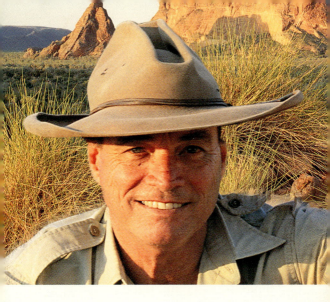

INTRODUCTION

When it comes to bush tucker, the one question that seems to pop up time and time again is 'How did Aboriginal people know what they could eat and what they couldn't eat?' Well, the answer is probably quite simple. Just like Europeans – or any other people for that matter – they used trial and error. The results of that trial and error might not always have been too pleasant. In fact, in some cases the result was probably deadly and I'm just a little glad to have been born down the track from those early days.

As many of our early explorers found, plants in Australia are often toxic. Yet in some regions where food wasn't always that plentiful, Aboriginal people found ways of treating certain plants to make them edible. This was usually a long and tedious process, often taking days. Even then, I reckon the food didn't always taste that great. But in a survival situation it would often have meant the difference between life and death. That knowledge about which plants are poisonous and how to make them safe to eat would no doubt have been acquired over a very long time.

Knowing how to identify edible plants is not that easy. Just because the birds can eat something, doesn't mean it's suitable for human consumption. You can't simply go up to a plant or bush and look at its colour, or the shape of the leaves, to determine if it can be eaten. Likewise, you can't just assume that a food that's a particular colour or shape is not edi-

Apricot figs (*Ficus leptoclada*) are red, sweet and pleasant tasting.

ble. Just think about your local fruit and vegetable shop, and how many species you would walk away from if you didn't want to eat anything red. No more strawberries, no more red apples, no more red capsicum, no more red cherries… and what about plums and grapes, where would they fit into the scheme of things? It's just the same with our native foods. You've got to know about individual plants.

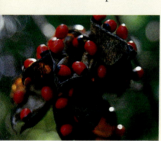

The red seeds of the gidgee gidgee (*Abrus precatorius*) are extremely poisonous.

Learn your country

I reckon the real answer is to take the time to learn what your country is all about and what the different environments have to offer. That way, you move out of the realm of guess-work and into the world of education. It means starting to appreciate the different climatic zones – the arid zone, the tropical rainforests and other environments. Once you start to understand a little more about these zones, you can start to grasp the many different types of vegetation. The wider the variety of vegetation in an environment, the greater the range of potential resources – and that means the more chance there is of finding bush foods. Once you start to understand the countryside, you might be surprised at the bush foods that can be found in some very unpromising environments.

Look to survive

Part of the learning process is a change in visual perspective. By that I'm referring to the way you look at the landscape – really, you should be looking *in* to the landscape, not *at* it. Literally 'reading' the landscape. That was one of the very first lessons I had to grasp once I started the learning process.

Aboriginal people dependent on their environment look at the landscape from a survival point of view – it certainly sharpens up your vision if you know you have to get your berries before the birds get them, find a particular vine that will lead to an underground tuber, or recognize an animal's footprints, if you're going to eat at all that day. This book isn't a survival guide, of course. It's a way of helping people learn more about their country.

Over the years, I've been lucky enough to spend a fair bit of time in the bush, and I've had some pretty good teachers sharing their knowledge of bush tucker. This field guide is an introduction to some of that knowledge – and once you start to learn, I reckon you'll be hooked. Each different region, each different season throws up something new. There's a tremendous amount to learn about and it's all out there, waiting to be discovered.

BUSH TUCKER

Aboriginal people have lived in this country for tens of thousands of years, and over that time they've found ways of surviving that reveal an intimate knowledge of their environment. Their understanding of indigenous plants goes way beyond just knowing what is edible. They used plants for tools and weapons, and for medicine and healing. They understood the seasons and the life cycle of plants and animals and the effect that had on their own survival.

This field guide brings together a range of plant foods as well as some reptiles (such as lizards), fish and shellfish, and a few of the more unusual bush foods such as grubs and honey ants.

The species included are mainly spread across northern Australia, because that's the country that I know best, but you'll find some of these foods in pockets all around Australia.

These small sweet honey ants (*Melophorus* sp.) were a prized bush tucker in the desert country.

Bush food is quite a fascinating subject, but there's still an awful lot we don't know about it. Many Australian foods contain toxins − some can make you pretty sick, others are deadly. What some people don't realise is that bush foods can also be rich in vitamins, trace elements and proteins. The Kakadu or billy goat plum (*Terminalia ferdinandiana*), for example, is the richest-known source of vitamin C in the world. The fruit was eaten in small quantities, almost like a medicine − and now we know why. That's just one of the secrets of bush food that we're beginning to understand.

Some of the foods included here would have been staples – foods that were a regular part of a traditional bush diet and could be relied upon from one year to the next. Some foods would have been a special treat; a delicacy. For example, something like sugar-bag, the native honey. Of course, in The Kimberley region honey was easier to find so it was a regular part of the diet. Other tuckers were just pickings – something to

In some regions, Aboriginal people enjoyed the nectar from the golden grevillea flowers (*Grevillea pteridifolia*).

snack on when it was briefly in season, or to eat when out hunting. That could be the sugary lerp scale found on some eucalyptus leaves, or the nectar from honey grevillea flowers, or gums found oozing from certain trees.

Different regions

Food habits and diets varied from one region to another. In fact, they varied from one tribe to another. Local custom and belief affected what was hunted and gathered. One tribe might have a particular animal as a totemic animal and would not harm it. For other tribes that animal might be fair game. Edible plants weren't always eaten. Toxic plants that were treated by some Aboriginal groups to make them edible were not touched by others.

In the northern coastal region there is an abundance of fish and shellfish for much of the year, and this would have made up a large part of the diet of Aboriginal people in the area. In the arid zone, out in the desert country, where the range of tuckers was more restricted, seeds and grasses were far more important.

Aboriginal people also ate a variety of animal foods when they were available, such as turtles, wallabies, lizards, emus, and so on. These were an essential part of the diet but they were always supplemented by plant foods.

Hunting and gathering

Whilst the men were the hunters, tracking large animals like wallabies and kangaroos, it was the women who collected the day-to-day tucker, such as roots, fruits, and small animals like lizards. Aboriginal women in particular have shared their knowledge with me over the years. They know what to look for, and they have an uncanny ability to remember where they've seen plants and whether they can expect to find them fruiting or flowering, depending on the season.

Women were also the ones who went out, with the children in tow, to find turtles, water snakes, shellfish and so on.

Preparing foods

Some bush foods were simply thrown on a fire, baked and eaten. Others required considerable preparation – soaking, leeching, grating, grinding and then cooking.

You must remember that traditionally, Aboriginal people did not cook in pots. Up Cape York way, bailer shells were sometimes used to warm water, but most food was cooked on coals, or in the ground beneath the coals. Sometimes food was wrapped in paperbark or leaves before cooking. Some animals, like kangaroos, were cooked in their skin; others, like turtles, were cooked in their shells.

Animals, such as lizards or kangaroos, were often cooked whole on a fire.

Aboriginal people did sometimes store or keep foods. When they were plentiful, nonda plums (*Parinari nonda*) might be buried in the ground for a few days or a few weeks, to help them ripen. In some regions, seeds were ground into a type of flour and then made into small 'johnny' cakes that could be carried.

Nonda plums (*Parinari nonda*) were sometimes buried for a few days or even a few weeks to help them ripen.

Bush medicine

Plants were also an important source of bush medicine. Most were applied, as rubs or poultices; or inhaled, for example by using crushed aromatic leaves. I guess you're fairly safe doing this, although some plants can cause an allergic skin reaction. I certainly don't recommend that you try making up bush medicines to drink, however.

BUSH TUCKER WARNING

■ This book is **not** a survival guide.

■ Plants are protected within national parks and you cannot pick fruits or flowers or otherwise interfere with plants.

■ When travelling through Aboriginal land, remember that permission is needed before fishing or gathering food.

■ Many species are difficult to identify.

■ Some plant foods are **highly toxic**. Some are **deadly**.

■ If in doubt, leave the plant alone.

How to use this book

Bush food categories

The bush foods in this field guide are listed under FLORA and FAUNA. Categories are colour-coded to help make them easier to locate.

FLORA

AQUATIC	plant that grows in water, e.g. water lily
GRASS	a plant like, or similar to, grass
HERB	a small plant, not woody
PALM	a usually tall, unbranched tree with a crown of fan-shaped leaves
PARASITE	a plant that exists by living in, or on, another plant without giving anything back
SHRUB	plant, usually less than 4–5 metres, without a tree-like trunk
TREE	a woody plant, usually with a main trunk
VINE	a climbing or sprawling plant

FAUNA

BIRD	warm-blooded vertebrate with feathers and wings
FISH	cold-blooded aquatic vertebrate with gills, and usually scales
INSECT/GRUB	small, air-breathing invertebrate; a grub is the bulky larva of certain insects
REPTILE	cold-blooded vertebrate, e.g. turtle, snake, lizard
SHELLFISH	aquatic animal (not a fish) having a shell, including crustaceans and molluscs e.g. oyster, crayfish

Finding an entry in the book

If you're in the field and trying to identify a tree, turn to the TREE category, under FLORA, and compare the picture and the text with the species.

If you already know the name and want more information about the plant or animal as a bush food, check the INDEX. Foods are listed under their common names as well as their scientific (Latin) names.

If a bush tucker name is in **bold** in an entry, that means it has its own entry in the Bush Tucker Field Guide.

What's it called?

The bush foods are listed in the category in alphabetical order by common name, with the scientific name (the Latin genus and species names) given as well.

Some alternative common names are given at the end of each entry.

Europeans had a habit of using names that related to plants they knew. That means you keep finding things called wild oranges, wild plums and wild figs all over the place. Aboriginal people have their own names for bush foods and these vary from one area to another, so I haven't tried to provide Aboriginal names.

Distribution maps

These give a broad view of where these tuckers can be found. The areas shown in dark pink indicate the distribution of the bush food. In some cases more than one species is included in the entry, so the range can look fairly wide, but specific species might be found only in small pockets through the distribution region.

Vegetation Types

Following is a brief explanation of the vegetation types of northern Australia that are mentioned in the entries.

Closed forest

Closed forests have dense canopies in the upper levels, which restrict light penetrating to the lower layers of vegetation. Few species are able to survive on the forest floor. The upper level can range from 5 m to 40 m tall. Closed forests are found in well-watered areas down the east coast, from Cape York to Tasmania. Closed forests along the Northern Territory coastal areas have fewer species and often a less complex structure, due to the extreme seasonal rainfall. Closed forests in northern Australia are also referred to as tropical rainforests, or sometimes monsoon forests. In Tasmania, southern New South Wales and south-east Victoria, the closed forests are known as temperate forests. Many mangrove communities can be defined as closed forests.

Open forest

Australia's open forests are dominated by *Eucalyptus* trees. The trees usually have straight trunks and canopy cover ranging from 30 to 70 per cent, though commonly it is at the lower end of that range. This type of forest can be found in tropical and temperate zones.

The category can be divided into tall open forest, open forest and low open forest. Tall open forest can support a dense under-layer of smaller trees or shrubs, tree ferns and grasses. Vegetation in open forests varies in the lower layers or storeys. These can range from hard-leaved shrubs in infertile soils to tropical grasses and herbs. Fires are common in open forests. The third sub-category, low open forests, tends to have less trees and a lower overall height.

Mangroves

Mangrove trees often form a **closed forest**. They thrive in the sheltered, muddy, tidal waters of the northern Australian coastline. Mangroves can grow as far south as Westernport, Victoria, but are most common in the tropical areas, where almost all of Australia's 30 known species grow.

Savannah

Savannah is a type of grassland, usually monotonous and uniform, typically unbroken by trees, and covering large areas of northern Australia.

Tropical savannah

Tall grasses, dominated by Mitchell grass (*Astrebla* sp.), cover rolling treeless plains.

Woodland

Woodlands in Australia are usually dominated by *Eucalyptus* trees, although sometimes by *Casuarina*, *Melaleuca*, *Acacia* and *Callitris* trees. Tetrodonta woodland, for example, is woodland dominated by the species *Eucalyptus tetrodonta*. Woodland trees are usually heavily branched with a fairly short trunk and a spreading canopy. Woodland is the main forest type in Australia. It occurs in all states, but varies in height, form and density of species. Broadly speaking, the denser forest forms grow in the moister areas; more sparse growth is common in drier areas.

Open woodland

Similar to woodland country, but featuring scattered low trees, which grow singly or in clumps, with hummock and tussock grasses creating an under-storey.

Tropical woodland

In tropical northern Australia, **woodland** is characterised by an under-storey of annual grasses, which can grow rapidly to a height of 3 m or more during the wet season.

Legend

The following explanations will help in identifying plant species.

Leaves

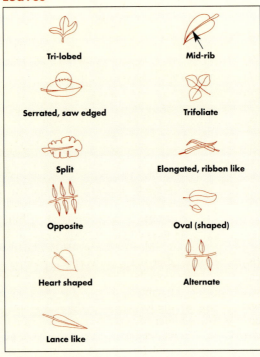

Tri-lobed

Mid-rib

Serrated, saw edged

Trifoliate

Split

Elongated, ribbon like

Opposite

Oval (shaped)

Heart shaped

Alternate

Lance like

Other features

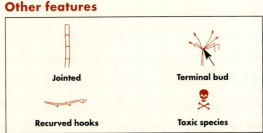

Jointed

Terminal bud

Recurved hooks

Toxic species

 ORIGINATING FROM SOUTH-EAST Asia, the lotus lily now occurs naturally in the wetland areas of tropical Australia. It can be found in billabongs and permanent lagoons. It is often mistakenly identified as a **waterlily** (*Nymphaea* spp.), but there are two major differences. The enormous leaves do not float on the water surface but stand some distance above the water. Secondly, the lotus seed pod is like a large cone with a number of visible chambers. In each chamber is a single seed about the size of a large peanut. The large, pink flowers have a yellow centre.

USES The seed pods can be cracked open and the seeds eaten raw. They have an excellent flavour, rather like a rich peanut taste. The older, more mature seeds can be roasted, crushed and used as a substitute for coffee granules. The younger leaves can be eaten raw or cooked. The roots of young plants can be cooked or if very young, eaten raw.

OTHER NAMES Sacred lotus, pink waterlily, red lily

NARDOO
Marsilea drummondii

NARDOO, A TYPE OF FERN, GROWS quite widely in Australia and is always found growing either in mud or in water itself. It is very similar in appearance to clover, with four small leaflets. Throughout the year it produces a small brown seed pod, about the same size as a split pea.

USES The plant was only used as a food resource by Aboriginal people in some areas. Depending on the season, the pods would be gathered in bulk and ground between two rocks to form a rough, yellow-coloured flour. This flour would be sifted to remove husks and cracked pod casings. Water would be added to the flour to produce a dough that was baked on hot coals. These 'nardoo cakes' have a rather bland taste, but supplied bulk and some nutritional value in the form of starch.

OTHER NAMES Clover fern

THE NYPA PALM ONLY GROWS IN very wet areas such as swamps and waterways, and prefers brackish water, so is only found around coastal areas. The palm resembles a short stunted coconut tree, growing 5–8 m high. At various stages throughout the year, the palm produces large nuts that look something like a fibrous woody pineapple. Each nut is made up of a number of wedge-shaped seeds, all joined to a central core, and each seed contains an edible white kernel.

USES The terminal bud of the palm tree is edible raw or cooked – although harvesting it will kill the palm. A sweet sap can be obtained by daily tapping the curved stem of the flower cluster shortly after it blooms. The kernels from the nut have a sweet taste. The long fronds of the palm were used for thatching and shelter construction in some areas.

OTHER NAMES Mangrove palm

SCURVY WEED
Commelina sp.

SCURVY WEED IS A GROUND-running vine found in the tropical and sub-tropical regions. It is prolific throughout the year and favours the moist ground areas beside creek lines and watercourses. The vine stem is jointed and attached to the ground by a series of roots that grow from these joints. A number of glossy green leaves grow at the terminal bud. Flowers are three-petalled and bright blue. The vine grows in patches, covering the ground with a grass-like matting.

USES As its common name suggests, this plant was sometimes used by early settlers as a green vegetable to ward off scurvy. The terminal bud of the vine is edible raw or cooked and has a lettuce–spinach taste.

A TALL GRASS–LIKE RUSH FOUND IN wetlands and along the edges of creeks and rivers. The leafless dark green strands are hollow. The spikerush is particularly favoured by magpie geese for constructing their floating nest systems. The strands can reach up to 2 m in height toward the end of the wet season. Edible underground 'chestnuts' or tubers, slightly larger than a golf ball, are white when young and dark brown when more mature.

USES Near the end of the wet season, from February to April, the rush would be dug up and the underground chestnuts collected. They were eaten raw or roasted. Spikerush foliage forms an excellent ground cover for shelter construction. Aboriginal people also used the stems as a medicine to help treat serious wounds. The rush was pulverised in water and allowed to stand for some hours, then the water was used as an antiseptic.

OTHER NAMES Water chestnut

WATERLILY
Nymphaea spp.

THE WATERLILY IS FOUND IN freshwater environs across northern Australia. The very large, smooth leaves float on water. Eye-catching, many-petalled flowers, which are held erect on stiff stems, vary in colour from white to pink to purple or blue. Seed pods are usually found just below the water's surface. They are a greenish-coloured berry, filled with thousands of tiny seeds. The lily also has underground bulbs.

USES The waterlily was an important part of the diet of Aboriginal people in northern areas. The bulbs and roots can be eaten after roasting on hot coals. The seed pods, which are slightly larger than a golf ball, can be eaten raw, or were sometimes roasted before removing the seeds. The stems of the lily were also roasted and chewed, or sometimes eaten raw. The leaves of the plant were crushed and rubbed over exposed areas of the body to prevent attack by leeches.

OTHER NAMES Giant waterlily

BAMBOO
Bambusa spp.

GRASS

BAMBOO IS ENDEMIC TO MANY areas in tropical northern Australia. It is commonly found in the wetland country, and along river and creek banks. It is a hardy clumping grass with a vigorous spreading root system and hollow jointed stems. It grows to a height of 15 m or more. The leaves are narrow, pointed and often bright green. Bamboo outcrops are frequently home to flying fox colonies as well as a wide range of reptiles. Bamboo is available throughout the year, although towards the end of the dry season it does tend to dry out and die off.

USES Although fresh young bamboo shoots can be boiled and eaten as a vegetable, as they are in South-East Asia, Aboriginal people do not appear to have used the plant as a food resource. However, in some areas they did use it to make spears and didjeridus.

BULRUSH
Typha domingensis, T. orientalis

THIS PLANT IS COMMONLY FOUND growing on the edges of lagoons and waterways. It is distinguished by its long, vertical flower spikes and strap-like green leaves. From October to January, new shoots emerge from the base. During April and May the shoots produce a yellow pollen.

USES The soft white part of the young shoot is edible. The flower spikes produce a yellow pollen. In some areas, the pollen was shaken from the flower stalks, collected and made into a rough flour that could be baked as small cakes. The brown and white down or fluff from the flowering spike can be used as a wound dressing. When bundled together, bulrushes provide a degree of buoyancy, and were useful as a flotation aid. The watery sap from the plant has been used as a protection against leeches.

OTHER NAMES Cat tail

CHAFF–FLOWER
Achyranthes aspera

THE CHAFF–FLOWER IS A THIN-stemmed weed, most often found growing in sandy soil across northern Australia. It grows up to a metre in height, with a long, flowering spike at the end of the stem. As they mature, the small seed pods form recurved hooks along the stem. The plant can usually be found throughout the year.

USES The young leaves can be boiled and eaten as a vegetable.

GIANT SPEAR GRASS
Heteropogon triticeus

THIS GRASS OCCURS MAINLY IN closed tropical woodland and open woodland environments, and is quite common across northern Australia. It gets its everyday name from the long upright canes, with seed heads that are spear-like in shape. When fully mature, towards the end of the wet season, the grass stems reach an average height of 2 m and make walking difficult. By April or May the grass is often knocked down by wind and rain.

USES The base of each grass stem is white in colour. This base can be chewed or sucked and has a pleasant, sweetish flavour similar to sugarcane. The fibrous remains of the stem or cane are not swallowed.

THIS GRASS–LIKE PLANT IS MOST often found beside tracks, creeks and other sunlit areas around tropical rainforest areas. It grows to a height of 2 m. The long grass-like blades are saw-edged and can easily cut the skin badly on contact. The terminal bud produces a flower–seed stalk. The seeds can be bright red, black, brown or grey in colour. When fully ripe, the seeds are hard and shiny.

USES The seeds were gathered by shaking the stem and collecting the fallen seeds. These seeds were then pounded and ground between two rocks, so as to produce a rough kind of flour. The flour was then baked as a damper and eaten.

OTHER NAMES Red-flowered saw-sedge

SPINIFEX
Triodia spp.

SPINIFEX IS THE HARSH, SPIKY GRASS commonly found throughout the drier regions of Australia. There are a number of different species, often difficult to distinguish from one another. The grass grows in hummocks, and the stems are sharply pointed. Seed heads are carried on stalks.

USES At certain times of the year, some species exude a sticky sap or resin which, when slowly heated, forms globules. These globules were collected and used as a form of bush glue or putty. Once the resin cools it becomes extremely hard. It was an important tool for Aboriginal people. As a bush medicine, young ground-runners were pulverised, soaked in water for a few hours, then the mixture used as an antiseptic for cuts and burns. The grass was practical for constructing shelters and using as windbreaks. As spinifex burns with a great intensity of heat it was also used to start fires.

THE ARROWROOT PLANT, USUALLY found behind sandy beaches or monsoon forests, is quite distinctive in appearance. The leaves of the ground plant are broad and a rich green in colour. During the later part of the wet season, it grows a tall erect stem with a cluster of hanging seeds and fine, trailing tendrils.

USES The small white seeds contained in the hanging seed pods were eaten raw and have a fairly bitter taste, if not properly ripe. No more than two pods of seeds should be eaten at one time, as they can be toxic. The major food source of the arrowroot is contained in the underground bulb. This white, potato-like bulb, found in soft loam soils, is fully developed from around January to August. The bulbs are highly toxic without extensive preparation. Aboriginal people would grate the bulb, soak it in several changes of water, and then cook the starchy plant to make it edible.

OTHER NAMES Polynesian arrowroot

AUSTRALIAN BUGLE
Ajuga australis

A HERB-LIKE PLANT, FAIRLY common in open forest areas in eastern Australia, where it can be found throughout the year. It has broad, fleshy leaves that are a greenish-grey colour, with a fine matting of tangled grey hair on both upper and lower sides. The leaves are slightly and irregularly indented along the edges. The plant produces small, spiky purple and mauve flowers from March to May. These flowers have irregular indentations along their petals, similar to those of the leaves.

USES Aboriginal people in some areas used the plant as a bush medicine. They would bruise and soak the leaves in hot water to make an infusion to bathe sores and boils.

BUSH CARROT
Eriosema chinense

THE BUSH CARROT INHABITS WET sandy areas, such as soaks at the base of rocky outcrops. It is difficult to find, however, as it is a small slender herb and not easy to distinguish from the weeds and grasses that also grow in these areas. It grows up to 50 cm high, with a single upright stem and narrow alternate leaves. The leaves are slightly furry. Small, flattened seed pods, which are also furry, grow towards the top of the stem. A small carrot-like tuber can be found several centimetres below the ground. The plant dies back in the dry season and the 'carrot' can be hard to locate.

USES The carrot could be eaten raw, but was considerably improved by roasting on hot coals. It was quite an important staple food in northern Australia.

OTHER NAMES Bush potato

PIG FACE
Carpobrotus spp.

PIG FACE IS COMMONLY FOUND growing around the coastal environs of Australia, favouring beaches and sand dunes. Some species grow well in the southern states. It is a ground-running creeper with extremely fleshy, three-sided leaves. The leaves grow opposite one another along the central stem. Purple flowers look a little like a daisy flower. Some species of pig face produce an edible elongated purple fruit.

USES The pulpy flesh of the fruit can be eaten raw. The fleshy succulent leaves of all species can be boiled and eaten as greens. As a bush medicine, the juice from the plant can be successfully applied to sandfly bites. A poultice of crushed leaves was sometimes applied to burns and scalds.

THIS SUCCULENT GROUND–CREEPER is common throughout Australia. It often grows around moist areas and water catchments, particularly in the central arid regions. The plant can spread up to a metre in diameter, with ground-running stems – that simply lie along the surface of the ground – radiating in all directions. Although basically bluish–green, the plant is also tinged with pink- or red-coloured stems. Often the young fleshy leaves are reddish as well. The small fruit or seed pods contain masses of minute black seeds. When the plant begins to dry out, the pods open up and release the tiny black seeds.

USES The seeds were an important food staple for desert Aboriginal tribes. The seeds could be gathered and saved until needed, or ground into a flour and baked into a rough cake. The fleshy leaves and shoots were eaten raw or cooked. Explorers and early settlers also cooked and ate the pigweed greens.

OTHER NAMES Purslane

THISTLE
Emila sonchifolia

THISTLE IS A PLANT OF OPEN SUNLIT areas, and is common around river banks and high rocky ground. It resembles a common garden weed in appearance, usually with a bunch of spearhead-shaped leaves at ground level, and tall thin stems to 60 cm high bearing small flower pods. The leaves have an 'eaten' appearance, with soft prickles around the edges.

USES The entire plant, including the root system, can be boiled and eaten as greens. It can also be eaten raw, and has a crisp lettuce-like taste. As a bush medicine, thistle leaves were boiled in water, and the liquid used to bathe patients with colds, flu and headache.

ALEXANDRA PALM
Archontophoenix alexandrae

PALM

THIS PALM IS RESTRICTED TO THE east coast of northern Queensland. It can be found growing in moist ground or beside watercourses, often in groups forming a small colony. The palms reach up to a height of 20 m. The trunk is slim except at the base, where it tends to bulge. When the palm is a few years old it produces masses of small red seeds that litter the ground.

USES The terminal bud, or 'cabbage', at the top of the trunk can be eaten, but as this kills the palm, Aboriginal people may have only cut the bud when food was in short supply. The 'cabbage', eaten raw after stripping away the leaf fronds, has a pleasant, crisp taste. Except in a survival situation, however, it should not be cut.

CABBAGE TREE PALM

Livistona spp.

A NUMBER OF RELATED CABBAGE palms inhabit tropical wet regions of Australia. These palms are particularly prominent in the closed tropical woodland regions of Cape York, Arnhem Land and The Kimberley. The trunk is straight and very rough. The long leaf stems often have recurved thorns on the underside. Each stem produces a large, tough, fan-shaped palm leaf.

USES The crisp white heart of the palm trunk, just below the apex or terminal bud, is edible raw or cooked. This pith has a slightly bitter, cabbage-like taste. Removing the terminal bud destroys the tree, however. The 'cabbages' were an important food for Aboriginal people.

A PALM FOUND IN THE CLOSED tropical woodland and tropical rainforest areas of Cape York Peninsula. The tree grows to around 10 m and has distinctive fronds with an almost circular fan-like appearance.

USES The terminal bud or cabbage of the palm is edible, however taking that bud kills the tree. At the base of the palm fronds is a hessian-like wrapping. Small birds often used this for nesting and Aboriginal people would look there for eggs. The fronds were sometimes used for shelter construction and thatching.

COCONUT PALM
Cocos nucifera

ALTHOUGH THE COCONUT PALM is not a native, it is now widely distributed along Queensland's northern coastline. When about seven years old, the palm starts to produce numerous large nuts, encased in a thick fibrous husk. When mature, the nuts turn brown and drop to the ground (a good reason not to camp under coconut palms).

USES The liquid (milk) inside the nut is tasty and nutritious. The fibrous husk can be removed by striking the nut downward onto a sharpened stake fixed into the ground, and levering the husk from the hard shell of the nut. The nut has three 'eyes'. If two of these are pierced, the milk can drain. The milk from the young green nuts can also be consumed. With green coconuts, the husk is simply sliced off using something like a machete. In young coconuts the flesh is soft, chewy and fibrous. The terminal bud or apex of the palm is also edible raw or cooked, however, this destroys the palm, so it should only be used in a survival situation.

CYCADS CAN BE FOUND IN MUCH OF Australia's tropical woodland country. They are related to plants that grew millions of years ago. They are very slow growing; some plants may be hundreds of years old. They look similar to tree ferns, however the fronds and the trunk are much harder and rougher in texture. The underside of the fronds have harsh recurved hooks, particularly around the base of the stem. From May to November, clusters of attractive large nuts are produced and hang from the terminal bud or apex of the palm. These nuts are extremely poisonous if they have not been treated. Many early explorers ate the cycad nuts and suffered the ill effects. The nuts are also poisonous to cattle.

USES The cycad is toxic and should not be eaten. The nuts however, provided a source of protein for Aboriginal people, who had an elaborate process of preparation. This included roasting the nuts, airing them, pounding them, washing them under running water for days and then baking them.

FAN PALM
Livistona inermis

THERE ARE A VARIETY OF *Livistona* palms in northern Australia and the fan palm is one species that is distributed right across the region. Unlike some palms, the *Livistona inermis* is quite small. The trunk is very thin and the tree only grows to about 2 m in height. Like other *Livistona* palms, each frond is on the end of a long arm or stem, which joins the trunk of the tree at the crown. This area where the stems join is called the heart or the terminal bud. The palm also produces small fruit that turn purple–black when ripe.

USES Aboriginal people would eat the terminal bud of the palm, raw or roasted. It sometimes has a slightly bitter taste, a little like cabbage. However, eating the heart of the palm does kill the tree. The berries are edible but don't taste very good.

SOLITAIRE PALM
Ptychosperma elegans

A PALM OF THE TROPICAL rainforest. It prefers the coastal lowland regions below 500 m altitude. The palm has a slim trunk and grows to a height of 15 m. Green flowers appear in large sprays. Small red to yellow fruit, attached to tough yellow stems or thongs, grow around the terminal bud area. The palms have two fruiting seasons: January to March and July to September.

USES The ripe red fruit can be eaten raw and has a sweet taste. The edible cabbage of the palm was sometimes eaten but this kills the plant.

BLOODWOOD APPLE
Cystococcus sp.

THESE ROUND WOODY GROWTHS can be found on the branches of a variety of eucalypts, including **bloodwood** trees (*Eucalyptus terminalis*), across a wide swathe of outback Australia. In some areas they are around the size of a golf ball, with a smooth light grey bark. In other places the galls are larger than cricket balls, with a dark, rough surface. When cracked open the galls reveal a hollow pink or white lining with an edible grub. The grub resembles a yellowish sac of moisture anchored to the lining at each end. The white inner lining, also edible, has a woody, coconut-like flavour. These galls or apples may be found at any time of the year.

USES The grub and lining were eaten raw.

OTHER NAMES Bloodwood gall, insect gall, bush coconut, bush apple

TREE ORCHID
Cymbidium canaliculatum

PARASITE

THE COMMON TREE ORCHID IS often found in open tropical wood-land areas, attached to branches of eucalyptus trees. The leaves of the tree orchid are always long, tapered and smooth. These fleshy sword-like leaves have a deep groove or V-shape running up the centre. From August to January bunches of attractive orchid flowers are produced, which can vary in colour from greenish-yellow, to white, through to reddish-brown. Pods hang in bunches from the plant during the wet season.

USES Once the pods turn brown, the kernel can be eaten raw. It has a taste similar to peanuts. The juice from the stems was used by Aboriginal people as a glue as well as a bush medicine. The juice was applied directly to wounds and in particular to burns.

OTHER NAMES Rock orchid, black orchid

☠ BRACKEN FERN
Pteridium esculentum

BRACKEN FERN IS FOUND IN MOIST shaded gullies and eucalypt forests. It has quite tough green fronds with stiff stems.

USES When used as a survival food, the young undeveloped fronds, or fiddle-heads, must be boiled prior to eating. They have an asparagus–like taste. Research has shown recently that prolonged consumption of bracken fern may cause cancer. The sap from the stems of young ferns was used by Aboriginal people to relieve the pain of insect stings. This was done by applying the sap directly to the affected area of skin.

SHRUB

THE BUSH RAISIN GROWS IN THE arid zone in Central Australia, favouring sandy soil environments. Like many bush tuckers of the desert, it produces a food crop shortly after rainfall. The bush grows to about 2 m high, and has broad, rough, very green leaves. The oval-shaped leaves grow opposite each other. The green bunches of berries produced by the bush turn black when fully ripe, as does the flesh inside. The bush raisin is often found growing as a 'regrowth' in burnt-out areas of the desert country.

USES The small black berries contain one inedible seed and a small amount of sweet flesh. They should only be eaten in small quantities as they can create a rash on the mouth. The leaves can be eaten raw and have an agreeable, very sweet taste.

OTHER NAMES Native currant, native citrus

CONKERBERRY
Carissa lanceolata

A SCRUBBY, TANGLED BUSH FOUND growing in sandy and sandy loam-type soils across northern Australia. The bushes grow to around 2 m in height. The elongated leaves are bright green, with new growth tinged yellow. There are quite long thorns. Small white flowers appear in autumn. From May to August small, oval-shaped fruit are produced. When picked, these berries exude a small dot of white sap as well as a general sticky feeling. The berries turn from green to red to dark purple–black when fully ripe.

USES The ripe berries have an agreeable sweet taste and can be eaten raw. The season is quite short, but Aboriginal people sometimes collected the dried berries from the ground and then soaked them before eating. The bark has been used as a bush medicine, being soaked in water to make a medicinal wash.

OTHER NAMES Konkleberry, bush plum

Alocasia macrorrhizos

SHRUB

THE CUNJEVOI IS EXTREMELY poisonous. It grows in rainforest and damp areas and can be found most of the year. It looks like a lily, with three or four very large, often heart-shaped leaves on the end of long fleshy stems. When cut, the stems give off a sticky clear sap. Flowers are yellowish in colour and perfumed. The red berries are not edible.

USES Aboriginal people ate the starchy roots of the plant, but only after extensive preparation. Untreated, the plant and the roots are extremely poisonous. Definitely do not eat this plant. The sap, if applied to the skin, is said to relieve the pain of the sting from the **giant stinging tree** (*Dendrocnide* spp.). The cunjevoi can often be found growing near the stinging tree. The sap was also used to relieve snake bite, stings from insects and stingrays. The leaves were crushed and washed in pools of water as a fish poison.

OTHER NAMES Spoon lily

EMU BERRY
Grewia retusifolia

EMU BERRY PLANTS FLOURISH IN open woodland and closed tropical woodland areas. The plant, looking like an overgrown weed, can grow to a height of one metre. A multitude of single stems usually sprout from the one location. The leaves, growing alternately on either side of the stem, are darkish dull green, saw-edged and covered with fine hairs. From April to September groups of shiny brown berries grow along the stems. Each berry has two, three or even four segments, each segment containing a large white stone.

USES The skin and thin layer of pulp around the white stone can be eaten raw, and tastes similar to stewed apples. The plant was known as a very effective bush medicine in northern Australia. The entire plant was crushed then boiled, and the broth drunk for the relief of colds, flu and diarrhoea. It was also used to bathe sore eyes.

OTHER NAMES Turkey bush, dog's balls, dysentery bush

See also **Giant emu berry**

THIS PLANT IS TOXIC. IT SHOULD not be eaten. A small shrub up to around 2.5 m, it is most often found on sandy soil in an arid environment, around sand dunes and especially near salt lakes. After rain, the plant produces small white flowers with fine purple lines in the throat. Soon after the flowers, green to black berries appear.

USES As its name suggests, this plant was used by Aboriginal people to poison emus. The leaves were pounded and soaked in a small catchment of water. When an emu came to drink at the waterhole, the narcotic in the water attacked the bird's nervous system and the stupefied bird would fall to the ground. The drug attacks the nervous system, but the birds could still be eaten after cooking. The water, however, was not suitable for human consumption for days or even weeks. The narcotic is sufficiently strong to affect even large animals such as cattle and camels.

OTHER NAMES Pituri bush

GIANT EMU BERRY
Grewia asiatica

GIANT EMU BERRIES CAN BE FOUND in open forest areas, along river flats and around rocky foothills. This is a small bush or tree with long arching canes. The leaves are apple-green in colour and broadly heart-shaped, up to 30 cm across with saw-toothed edges. Dead sticks from the previous year's growth often remain attached to the plant. The berry-like fruit are produced at the base of the arching canes on low bushy plants, or along the branches. They are usually two-lobed and sparsely covered with short hairs, and appear during the wet summer months. The fruit turn from yellow-green to a dark purple-red when ripe, and are around 1.5 cm in diameter. They contain an inedible white stone.

USES The berries can be eaten raw and taste like fresh green apples. The roots were also used to make a bush medicine.

See also **Emu berry**

SHRUB

THE GIANT STINGING TREE CAN inflict an extremely painful wound that may last or re-occur for up to several weeks or months. The tree is found in rainforest areas, growing in sunlit areas such as beside track and river systems. The large heart-shaped leaves appear dull green and are covered in very fine poisonous hairs. Contact with the leaves or even the trunk will inflict a severe sting which can penetrate clothing. The fine hairs from dead leaves may be inhaled and can cause severe irritation to the eyes, throat and mouth. There are a number of so-called 'cures'; their effectiveness seems to vary from person to person. One cure is as follows: firmly apply adhesive Elastoplast over the affected area. Once it's strongly attached, quickly rip off the plaster, thereby removing the stinging hairs from the skin. At various times during the year, the tree produces purplish-red fruit clusters.

USES The fruit are edible but should be left alone due to the danger of being stung.

OTHER NAMES Stinger, gympie gympie

GREAT MORINDA
Morinda citrifolia

SHRUB

THE MORINDA IS ALWAYS FOUND close to the coastline in tropical areas. It looks more like a bush than a tree and is generally low set with large, broad, glossy green leaves. These leaves grow opposite each other. The flowers are small, white and sweet-scented. The fruit is elongated in shape, with irregular depressions on the outer surface. The fruit turns from green to whitish-yellow when fully ripe. The morinda appears to produce fruit throughout the year. The fruit is quite unmistakable, with a translucent flesh, many brown seeds and a powerful aroma similar to rancid cheese.

USES The fruit is eaten raw or cooked and the young leaves are also edible. Many Aboriginal people used the morinda as a cure for coughs, colds and flu. Young leaves and fruit were crushed and inhaled or rubbed on the chest. The fruit also has a slight anaesthetic effect on the throat when eaten.

OTHER NAMES Cheese fruit

LOLLY BUSH
Clerodendrum floribundum

LOLLY BUSH IS USUALLY FOUND IN the arid zone, growing alongside water sources such as soaks and rock-holes. It also occurs on coastal plains and sometimes behind coastal dunes, where it can be rather spindly. Because the bush grows in well-drained soil with a permanent supply of moisture, it can be a good water indicator in some areas. The low squat bush has bright green, oval-shaped leaves. During the wet season, it carries bunches of long white flowers with protruding 'whiskers', followed by red and black seed heads (which are not eaten). The stems are usually hollow.

USES The main root was dug up, roasted and then eaten, leaving the fibrous inner portion. The roots have a starchy taste. Aboriginal people also used the dried sticks of lolly bush for friction fire-lighting. This was done by rubbing a sharp piece of dried hardwood across the lolly bush sticks (a practice not easily mastered). In some areas the leaves were used for medicinal purposes.

SHRUB

THE MANGROVE FERN IS WIDELY spread throughout northern Australia and is the only fern found growing in the mangrove environment. It can reach over a metre in height and is often found covering large areas around the creek lines and waterways that feed the mangroves. It tends to grow in clumps and has thick, dull green, leathery leaves.

USES As a food source the mangrove fern was not particularly popular with Aboriginal people. The black underground roots or stems – poisonous unless carefully prepared – were dug up, skinned, washed in fresh water, and finally roasted on hot coals.

MISTLETOE IS A PARASITIC SHRUB, which favours Australia's arid inland areas. It is commonly found growing on the trunk and branches of wattle and eucalypt trees. The leaves are often oval-shaped and fleshy to touch. Throughout the year, red trumpet-shaped flowers are produced, as well as masses of berries. The berries, about the size of a domestic pea, are darkish in colour. Inside each berry is a seed, surrounded by a sticky grey-coloured mucous membrane.

USES The skin and flesh of the berry can be eaten raw and have a pleasant, sweetish taste. The berries have an easily identified characteristic – once they are in the mouth, it is literally almost impossible to 'spit out the seed' because of the extremely sticky texture of the pulp and the way in which the pulp is attached to the seed. Aboriginal people would eat the fruit without chewing so they wouldn't stick to the tongue.

NATIVE GOOSEBERRY
Physalis minima

SHRUB

THE NATIVE GOOSEBERRY IS FOUND growing in coastal and riverbank environments, generally in semi-shaded areas, and quite often as an understorey regrowth shrub. It is very similar in appearance to the introduced variety, the **cape gooseberry** (*Physalis peruviana*). The bush only grows to a height of about 1.5 m, has soft green leaves and cream flowers. Throughout the year small berries are produced. These berries are encased in a paper-thin, almost transparent capsule. As the capsule ages it dries to a fawn colour, the berry inside matures, turning yellow when fully ripe. When ripe, the berries are particularly popular with birds.

USES The berries can be eaten raw and have a pleasant sweet but tangy taste.

NATIVE KAPOK BUSH
Cochlospermum fraseri

THE NATIVE KAPOK BUSH IS commonly seen in northern Australia, particularly in the Northern Territory and The Kimberley. It is found in tropical woodland areas but seems to favour the drier country, particularly rocky ground. The bush is rather spindly, occasionally reaching 5–6 m in height but usually only growing to 3 m. Eye-catching bright yellow flowers are produced from about May to November. From July to December green pods hang from the branches. Within these pods is the 'kapok' or fluffy 'cotton'.

USES The roots of the younger trees were roasted on hot coals and eaten. The yellow petals were eaten raw in small quantities, and the inner bark from the trunk and roots was twined to form a strong bush string. The young, dried-out stems of the tree were used by Aboriginal people to make fire sticks. The 'kapok', when fully dry, provides a good tinder for lighting fires.

OTHER NAMES Native kapok

NATIVE ROCK FIG
Ficus platypoda

THE NATIVE ROCK FIG OFTEN appears as a stunted green bush, growing on the side of rocky hills or outcrops, or near permanent water-holes. The main trunk and branches are thin and spindly. The green leaves are leathery. At various times during the year, depending on rainfall, marble-sized fruit are produced. The fruit turn from yellow to reddish-brown or black when fully ripe and are very soft to touch. When split open, the fruit reveals a seeded centre similar to the cultivated fig. Like all figs, a dot of white sap appears when fruit or leaves are plucked from the tree.

USES The figs are edible raw and have a dry, slightly sweetish taste. The trailing root system can sometimes indicate the presence of water pockets in rock crevices, particularly in arid areas. As the roots often penetrate deep crevices, the water may be a long way down. These figs were a favoured plant food, especially for desert tribes. Dried figs were sometimes collected and ground into a paste to eat.

OTHER NAMES Desert fig, wild fig

ALTHOUGH INTRODUCED, THIS bush is now found in even the most inaccessible areas of northern Australia. In the drier regions the native rosella is often found growing beside creek lines or along riverbanks. The low, shrubby bush looks almost like an overgrown weed and grows to about a metre in height. The attractive large yellow flowers with their dark red centres are a distinctive feature, and are usually produced after rainfall. From March to July young buds appear along the stem and branches. To some extent the seasonal period is dependent upon rainfall and may be slow to produce the edible buds following a 'late' wet season. The buds have a thick, crisp casing, which is dark red in colour, similar to a toffee apple. Other species of hibiscus do not have this casing.

USES The casing around the buds can be eaten raw and has a pleasant acidic taste. The casings are also an important source of moisture, containing up to 85 per cent water.

OTHER NAMES Native hibiscus

RAGAH
Flueggea virosa

THIS PLANT IS FOUND IN OPEN AND close tropical savannah areas. It takes the form of a low-growing, multi-stemmed bush. It is easily mistaken for a weed, not unlike lantana in appearance. The leaves are around 5 cm long and 3 cm wide, and have prominent light-coloured veins. Flowers are tiny and yellow to cream. During the wet season, ragah bears masses of very small white berries, in clusters along the stems. Each berry contains a number of small seeds.

USES The berries and seeds can be eaten raw. The very soft berries have a sweet taste and a high water content. The leaves were used for medicinal purposes, for various internal and external ailments.

OTHER NAMES White berry bush, white raisin

Ruby Saltbush
Enchylaena tomentosa

THERE ARE SEVERAL SPECIES OF saltbush in the arid zones of Australia. The plant grows to a height of just under a metre and often looks more like a stunted shrub than a bush. In the open country it is quite common and is frequently found growing in the partly shaded areas of large trees. The bush has small succulent leaves that are slightly silvery in colour. From a distance this gives the saltbush a blue or grey appearance. After rainfall, the bush produces masses of small edible ruby-red fruit. These berries are flattish in shape and turn bright red when completely ripe.

USES The berries can be eaten raw and are juicy and sweet-tasting. The young fresh leaves of the saltbush, which are quite fleshy, can be boiled and used as a vegetable substitute.

OTHER NAMES Creeping saltbush

SANDPAPER FIG, SWEET
Ficus opposita

THIS SANDPAPER FIG IS FOUND throughout the tropical woodland and stringybark forests of northern Australia. The rather spindly bush often grows to around 2 m, though it can sometimes be taller. It may have around four to six stems or branches emerging from the one ground location. The leaves always grow opposite one another. The leaves are quite stiff and the surface of the leaves is very rough, like sandpaper. From April to September crops of fruit are produced. When fully ripe and mature, the figs are about the size of a marble, jet-black in colour and very soft. Like all figs, a dot of milky sap appears on the skin of the fruit when freshly picked from the stem.

USES The figs can be eaten raw and are pleasantly sweet. Aboriginal people often used the leaves as a type of sandpaper, to smooth wooden spear shafts and so on. Various parts of the bush were used for medicinal purposes.

OTHER NAMES Sweet sandpaper fig

NATIVE GINGER CAN BE FOUND IN tropical rainforest areas, particularly on the verges of the forest or sunlit locations. The single-stemmed cane produces broad, glossy green leaves, and the canes grow in bunches up to 3 m long. At the base of the plant are the young tips of the underground stem. These protrude to a height of about 10 cm. There are two types of edible 'tips' or 'stems', one deep red and pointed, the other vivid green and cactus-like. These 'tips' appear from November to April. The plant also produces edible blue berries.

USES The berries can be eaten raw and have a slight ginger–pepper taste. The root system can be eaten after boiling but removing the root can destroy the plant so it should not be touched. The 'tips' contain an edible seedy pulp, with a flavour like fruit salad. The seeds are discarded or crushed and used as a spice. The leaves of the plant may be used for wrapping food prior to cooking.

OTHER NAMES Native ginger

WILD ORANGE

Capparis spinosa var. *nummularia*

THIS WILD ORANGE TENDS TO grow in red sandy soil or gravelly soil, usually in association with flood plains and creek or river beds. It is a low spiny scrambling shrub, about 1.5 m high. The bushes occur individually or as part of a small group. The oval-shaped leaves are grey-green in colour. The branches and twigs have a number of recurved thorns. The delicate tasselled flowers are usually white or cream, although pink and purple flowers have been recorded. From November to May green fruit are produced. These fruit have well-defined external ribs, running from the base to the apex. The fruit turns yellow on ripening and then splits open to reveal a number of hard black seeds embedded in a yellow pulp.

USES The fruit pulp is edible raw and has a taste and texture similar to mango. When in season, the fruit is particularly favoured by ants and birds.

OTHER NAMES Wild passionfruit, caper bush

WILD RASPBERRY
Rubus rosifolius

THE WILD RASPBERRY IS OFTEN found by the margins of tropical rainforests, beside creeks and tracks. It will grow only in sunlit areas. The bush produces a number of arching canes to a height of 2–3 m. The leaves of the dense bush are bright green, saw-edged and grow opposite each other. The bush has small white flowers followed by attractive red berries. The edible berries are in season from June to October.

USES The berries have a dry but sweetish taste. Early settlers and colonists used the berries to make jam. Old dried leaves, boiled in water, produce a tea that has a tannin content. This tea was sipped to relieve the symptoms of diarrhoea.

OTHER NAMES Rainforest raspberries, roseleaf raspberry, forest bramble

WILD TOMATO
Solanum echinatum

THIS SHRUB IS POISONOUS. This small prickly shrub can be found in rocky or sandstone country in well-drained soil. It grows to a height of about a half a metre. Like many *Solanum* species it produces a small, purple-coloured flower. The stems of the bush as well as the small tomato-like fruit are covered in fine sharp thorns. The wild tomato can be quite poisonous, depending on seasonal factors.

USES Like some other species of *Solanum*, this wild tomato is poisonous and should not be eaten. Some species of *Solanum* were certainly important foods for Aboriginal people in Central Australia. However, as it is difficult to distinguish the edible variety from the highly toxic variety, I recommend that people do not consider touching the *Solanums*, unless with an experienced bush tucker guide who can safely identify the species.

WITCHETTY BUSH
Acacia kempeana

IN THE MORE ARID REGIONS OF Australia, this bush often forms a major part of the landscape. Its distinctive shape and structure make it easily recognisable. Rarely does it have any sort of trunk, but rather a number of erect branches or stems that originate from a common base at ground level. The leaves, which form a rather dense crown on top of the bush, are smooth, broad and grey-green in colour. Seed pods are flat and dry. The roots of the bush frequently harbour the tasty and prized **witchetty grub** (*Cossidae* sp.)

USES Aboriginal women would dig away the soil from around the base of the bush to see the roots. Roots that harbour a grub have a very distinct and distorted bulge, indicating the exact location of the grub. The seeds of the witchetty bush, like those from many other acacias, were nutritious and an important food source in arid areas. They were ground into a flour and then cooked.

APRICOT FIG
Ficus leptoclada

A TROPICAL RAINFOREST TREE THAT can be found on the east coast of northern Queensland. It favours sun-lit areas on the edge of the forest. The tree is densely foliated and grows to a height of 5–10 m. The leaves are dark green and roughish on the upper surface. The fruit, only slightly larger than a domestic pea when fully grown, is produced in bunches from March to July. The fruit ripens from yellow to red and, like a domestic fig, is packed with small seeds inside the skin casing. When picked from the tree, a small white dot of sap will appear on the fruit stem.

USES The complete fruit, including the skin, was eaten raw. It has a pleasant sweet flavour.

BATWING CORAL TREE
Erythrina vespertilio

 FOUND IN BOTH INLAND AND coastal areas of northern Australia, often beside creeks and watercourses. This tree gets its common name from the distinctive two-lobed leaf shape, resembling a bat in flight. The trunk has greyish or yellowish corky bark with scattered thorns. Clusters of bright orange–red flowers in the dry season are followed by brown bean-like pods containing bright orange or red bean seeds. In dry locations this tree may drop all but a few of its leaves.

USES The seeds and the bark of the tree contain alkaloids and are quite poisonous. The root system is sometimes dug up and drained for drinkable water. When stripped of the outer bark, the roots could also be chewed or eaten raw to provide moisture. When dry, the wood is easily carved and Aboriginal people traditionally used it to make water-carrying vessels or coolamons. They also used the tree to make a bush medicine.

OTHER NAMES Cork tree, coral tree

BILLABONG TREE
Carallia brachiata

THIS IS A SMALL TO MEDIUM-SIZED tree, found growing beside watercourses such as creeks and billabongs. It grows to about 5 m in height. The bark of the trunk is deeply grooved and has a cork-like texture. The leaves are dark green, oval-shaped, with a waxy texture. During November and December the tree produces masses of small, edible berries, which turn from green to red and sometimes to black when fully ripe.

USES The ripe dark red or black fruit, which has a sweet taste, was eaten raw. The presence of this tree is a good indication of fresh water nearby. The bark was sometimes pounded and then boiled, to make a poultice for skin irritations and itches.

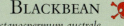

A LARGE TROPICAL RAINFOREST tree, often found along river and creek levees. It can easily be identified by the distinct cucumber-like aroma that comes from the crushed leaves. From May to October the tree produces large, attractive bean pods, which split in half to reveal up to six brown beans embedded in a white pith. The split pods resemble miniature canoes.

USES The large seeds in their raw state are extremely poisonous and, unless fully treated, produce severe stomach cramps. The seeds were an important food for Aboriginal people, who carried out extensive preparation before eating them. The seeds were first baked on hot coals then ground into a rough flour and washed in running fresh water for a minimum of ten days. This 'flour' was then baked into a type of damper. The taste of the finished product was extremely bland even after the lengthy preparation. Do not attempt to taste these seeds.

OTHER NAMES Moreton Bay chestnut

BLOODWOOD
Eucalyptus terminalis

TREE

A COMMON GUM TREE OF THE drier areas of Australia, occurring in open woodland, hilly country, and occasionally on flood plains of the larger rivers. It can grow to 15 m high but is usually smaller. The bark is greyish and rough. Attractive clusters of pale yellow blossoms are followed by large, vase-shaped gum nuts about 2 cm long. The dark red, gum-like sap often seeps from wounds in the trunk.

USES The blossoms produce a sweet nectar and can be dunked in a mug of water to produce a sweet, nutritious drink. The **native bee** (*Trigona* spp.) often builds its hive in the bloodwood. Edible **lerp scale** (*Psylla* spp.) is often found on the leaves of the bloodwood. The main fork of the trunk sometimes catches rainwater in a hollow, which can be drunk in an emergency. The sap was mixed with water and taken in small doses to relieve general sickness and diarrhoea. It was also used as an anti-septic and for tanning animal skins.

OTHER NAMES Desert bloodwood

A DISTINCTIVE TROPICAL RAINFOREST tree, often found in well-watered rainforest areas, particularly beside rivers and streams. It is tall with buttressed roots, and finely serrated leaves that turn red before falling. The small, vivid blue fruits appear around December to February. This fruit, about 2–3 cm in diameter, is mostly filled by a large, circular and deeply pitted stone. The first sign of a quandong tree is often the bright blue fruit being carried along waterways and streams.

USES The thin layer of greenish-coloured flesh and blue skin was eaten raw and has a slightly sour taste. Blue quandongs are not particularly nutritious.

OTHER NAMES Silver quandong

BOAB TREE
Adansonia gregorii

A WELL-KNOWN FEATURE OF THE Kimberley landscape, although the boab is recorded well into the Northern Territory. The tree grows to around 15 m. The trunk appears large and swollen and the branches twisted and deformed. The boab drops all its leaves during the dry season, giving it a stark appearance and accentuating the large pods. Flowers are white and fragrant. From April to July, large oval or sometimes round woody pods or nuts are produced.

USES The pods contain a bulky white pith that is edible, and has a pleasant, powdered-milk taste. It is exceptionally nutritious. The root of the tree, if cut, provided a source of moisture. The pith of the trunk is also heavily laden with water. To extract this water, the pith was cut into small pieces and squeezed or chewed.

OTHER NAMES Baobab, bottle tree

BRAMBLE WATTLE
Acacia victoriae

BRAMBLE WATTLE IS WIDESPREAD across the outback, and favours open scrubland and grassland, particularly around creek lines. It is a multi-stemmed bush, growing to a height of about 2 m. The foliage is usually blue–green and the bark of the branches is smooth, with the upper ends a vivid green colour. From October to December, masses of papery seed pods are produced, each one containing four to six brown seeds.

USES Like other acacias, the seeds are nutritious and were an important food source for Aboriginal people. The young green seeds were often eaten raw. Once the seeds began to ripen and become hard and brown, they were ground up to make a very basic sort of flour. This was made into small cakes and baked on hot coals or rocks. This wattle also produces a clear edible sap or gum, often found in globules on the main trunk.

OTHER NAMES Prickly wattle

BURDEKIN PLUM
Pleiogynium timorense

A LARGE, SOLID TREE FOUND IN open woodland and closed tropical woodland areas, particularly in coastal regions. It can grow to 20 m and has rich green, oval-shaped leaves. From April to October it produces a dark purple–black fruit, 3–4 cm across and squat in shape. The woody seeds or stones of the plums resemble miniature pumpkins. They are often found littering the ground beneath the parent tree throughout the year.

USES The fruit is acidic but quite pleasant to taste. It must be completely ripe before being eaten. Aboriginal people would bury the plums underground for several days to help ripen the fruit. The bark and roots of the tree were crushed and washed in small waterholes and streams as a 'fish poison'. The fish become stunned and float to the surface, but the flesh of the fish is unaffected.

BUSH BANANA
Musa acuminata

THE BUSH BANANA, WHICH resembles the cultivated species in appearance, is found in tropical rainforest regions, usually in sunlit and well-watered areas such as forest fringes and creek banks. It has a smooth-skinned fleshy trunk and broad, rich green leaves. The fruit is slender and often small, containing a large number of inedible black seeds.

USES The pulp can be eaten raw but is best cooked. The purple hanging flower or pod, the central heart of the trunk, and the young ground shoots were all cooked and eaten. The fruit has a slightly sweet taste and a sticky texture. The leaves were sometimes used to wrap food before it was cooked. The clear, sticky sap of the trunk was used as an antidote for the **giant stinging tree** (*Dendrocnide excelsa*), by applying the clear sap directly to the affected area of skin.

OTHER NAMES Native banana

TREE

BUSH GUAVA
Eupomatia laurina

THIS SMALL TREE IS FREQUENTLY found beside waterways in dense tropical woodland and coastal rainforest areas. When crushed, the glossy green leaves exude a mango-like aroma. From April to September the tree produces a fruit that looks like a large eucalyptus pod or 'gum nut'. The fruit becomes soft and smelly as it ripens.

USES The sticky pulp was eaten raw, and the bitter seeds discarded. The ripe, yellowish-coloured fruit has a hot spicy taste similar to pepper or nutmeg. The inner bark of the tree was sometimes used as a substitute for twine.

OTHER NAMES Native guava, bolwarra

BUSH LEMON
Citrus limon

TREE

THE WILD BUSH LEMON IS commonly found in the rainforest areas of north Queensland, often growing near creeks and rivers, or near old mining camps. Although originally introduced into the area it is now so widely spread that it is considered a local bush food in its own right. It resembles other cultivated citrus in appearance, but it has thorns that are extremely long and extremely sharp. The yellow fruit grows to about the size of a large domestic orange and has a rough, warty skin.

USES The skin is easily peeled using the fingers only. The lemons have a very sour but refreshing taste.

OTHER NAMES Native lemon

CANDLE NUT
Aleurites moluccana

A DISTINCTIVE TROPICAL RAINFOREST tree, up to 20 m high. The leaves are tri-lobed, and when young are covered with a white–silvery bloom, which gives the tree a shimmering appearance. During February, March and April the tree produces a large number of green pods, about 5–6 cm in diameter. The pods, which fall to the ground, contain up to four very hard nuts. These nuts can be found scattered for up to six months after podding.

USES The white kernel looks and tastes like the macadamia or Queensland nut. When raw, the nuts are very oily and have a potent laxative effect. Roasting the nuts neutralises this effect, improves the taste, and makes it easier to extract the nut from the shell. The nuts were a popular food with north Queensland Aboriginal tribes. The raw white kernels will burn to produce a slightly sooty, candle-like flame.

OTHER NAMES Carie nut (Indonesian name)

CASSOWARY GUM
Acmena hemilampra

THIS TREE IS MOST OFTEN FOUND along watercourses, in tropical rainforests, and vine-thicket areas behind coastal mangroves. The tree grows up to 30 m, with a rich, dark-green foliage. Young leaves are a fawn colour. The leaves grow opposite one another. From April to the end of August the tree produces massive clusters of globular, white-coloured berries. During this period the tree often looks as if it is covered in snow. The fruit is about 1.5-2 cm in diameter and contains a single large seed.

USES The crisp white flesh of the fruit can be eaten raw and has a pleasant, sweet-sour taste. The seeds should be discarded. These fruit are not especially nutritious, but were a popular bush tucker in northern Queensland.

OTHER NAMES Broad-leaved lilly pilly

CLUSTER FIG
Ficus racemosa

A TALL, THICK–SET, SPREADING TREE found in tropical rainforest and closed tropical woodland areas. The trees are frequently found near watercourses and shaded valleys. Clusters of figs grow along the trunk and main branches, and range from green to bright red, depending on the degree of maturity. On the outer skin are a number of small dots that form fine lines. Inside, the figs contain masses of seeds. There are two fruiting seasons: February to April, and July to November.

USES The fruit is similar in flavour to cultivated figs. It often harbours small insects and grubs; however, it is quite edible and of excellent quality. The inner wood of the branches was used as a bush medicine. It was scraped into warm water and the liquid drunk to relieve diarrhoea. Although not especially tasty, these figs provided a regular source of food for Aboriginal people living in various parts of northern Australia.

COCKY APPLE
Planchonia careya

A DISTINCTIVE TREE, COMMON IN closed and open tropical woodland in northern Australia. The cocky apple has twisted branches, oval-shaped leaves and elegant flowers. From October until the end of April it produces attractive pink and white tasselled flowers, which wither and drop to the ground within a few hours of sunrise. The broad green leaves turn to orange and red as they age. The greenish fruit is shaped like a lemon, with an unusual green 'whisker' projecting from one end.

USES The fruit's fleshy pulp is edible raw or roasted. The roots and bark of the tree contain saponin, and were pulverised and used as a fish poison. The inner portion of the trunk bark was used to make a strong twine. The tree was also important as a bush medicine for Aboriginal people. Pulverised roots were used as a poultice for the relief of infections, wounds as well as general skin irritations and complaints.

OTHER NAMES Native pear, wild quince

COOLIBAH
Eucalyptus microtheca

THE COOLIBAH, A WHITE-BARKED eucalyptus, is found growing beside creek lines and waterways. It bears rich green leaves, with a prominent central vein or mid-rib, which is often yellow in colour. The lower part of the main trunk may have the flaked remains of the previous bark growth, usually grey in colour.

USES Aboriginal people used the branches and leaves as a fish poison. The branches were cut, dried, then crushed and placed in a waterway. Gradually the water turned blackish-brown. The fish would be stunned and float to the surface, where they could easily be caught by hand. The roots of the coolibah were used to provide drinking water. After being dug from the ground the roots were cut into short lengths, stored vertically and allowed to drain. The bark of the tree trunk was also pounded to make a poultice to use as a snake-bite cure.

OTHER NAMES River ghost gum

THE GNARLED AND STUNTED corkwood favours open savannah and hilly country in Central Australia. Its stubby bunches of spindly leaves can resemble long spikes with sharp pointed ends, or drooping bootlaces. The bark is heavy and deeply fissured, grey in colour, though often blackened by bushfires. The heavy wooden seed pods remain on the tree for a long time. Corkwood trees usually flower in the wintertime, or occasionally after rain, producing bunches of white to yellow bottle-brush type flowers up to 20 cm long.

USES Nectar is collected from the heavily laden blossoms by 'bumping' the flowers over a container, or dipping them in a mug of water to produce a sweet nutritious drink. This is best done early in the morning before evaporation and the birds have taken their toll. Aboriginal people also used the corkwood as a bush medicine, rubbing ash from the burnt bark onto skin sores.

OTHER NAMES Hakea

COTTON TREE
Hibiscus tiliaceus

A SMALL TREE MOST COMMONLY found growing in coastal regions of tropical and sub-tropical Australia. It has heart-shaped, dark green leaves which develop fine silky hairs on the underside, creating a lighter appearance. Large yellow flowers with a dark red throat can be seen throughout the year.

USES The flowers and young leaves are edible, raw or cooked. The inner bark of the tree was used by Aboriginal people as a cure for ulcers and as an antiseptic for wounds. The bark was soaked in water, then the liquid used to bathe wounds. In some areas, a warm poultice of crushed leaves was applied to wounds or ulcers. The inner bark strands can be twined to make a strong string. The rough bark was boiled and used as a soap substitute. Straight shafts of the wood were dried in the sun and used for spears and fire sticks.

OTHER NAMES Yellow hibiscus, beach hibiscus

DAVIDSON PLUM
Davidsonia pruriens

A SMALL, TROPICAL RAINFOREST tree, which grows to around 10 m. The elongated leaves are dark green, and serrated along the edges. The fruit, a similar size and purple colour as domestic plums, grow in drooping bunches from August to January. The fruit is often seen littering the forest floor. The leaves and sometimes the fruit are covered with fine brown hairs that can cause skin irritation. Rub the hairs from the plum using large leaves found in the area. Clothing, handkerchiefs or hands should not be used for this task. The fruit has a deep red flesh that surrounds two flattish seeds or stones.

USES The juicy red flesh can be eaten raw and has a very sour, acidic taste. If you are able to get the fruit from a cultivated tree, the plums make excellent preserves and jam.

OTHER NAMES Sour plum

DESERT OAK
Allocasuarina decaisneana

DESERT OAKS ARE RESTRICTED TO specific arid areas around Central Australia. They are quite prominent and easily identified. Typically, the trunks are straight, thick and sturdy. The foliage, like that of a she-oak, has long, thin, drooping leaves like strands of hair. The foliage is quite dense, so they provide excellent shade.

USES The roots of the tree were sometimes used as a source of water. They were dug up, cut into short lengths, about half a metre, and drained overnight into a container. Where the branches join the main trunk of the tree, cracks and deep crevices often develop, creating small water catchments, which are well protected from the evaporative effects of the sun. Burnt ash from the leaves was used by Aboriginal people as a medicine. It was rubbed on open sores and cuts. The sweet white substance that often exudes from the 'oak apples' or 'cores' was eaten to relieve the light-headed feeling associated with water deprivation.

OTHER NAMES Desert she-oak

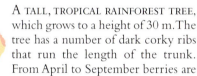

A TALL, TROPICAL RAINFOREST TREE, which grows to a height of 30 m. The tree has a number of dark corky ribs that run the length of the trunk. From April to September berries are produced. These fruit turn from green to dark purple to black when they are completely ripe. The berries contain at least two kidney-shaped seeds and can be found littering the rainforest floor.

USES The dark flesh was eaten raw and has a mild acidic taste. Aboriginal people would collect the ripe fruit after it had fallen to the ground.

OTHER NAMES Black plum

EMU APPLE TREE
Owenia vernicosa

A SMALL TO MEDIUM-SIZED TREE, up to 12 m tall, usually found in open forest and woodland. The tree can look a little like an iron bark or **bloodwood** tree (*Eucalyptus terminalis*), but on closer inspection the leaves are quite different. They are pinnate (herringbone) and hang down like a weeping willow. Round nuts grow on long stalks from the terminal shoot. The hard, inedible nuts are produced from May to August. Another species, *Owenia acidula*, also sometimes known as emu apple, produces an edible fruit.

USES The bark was used by Aboriginal people as a fish poison. The bark was pounded, then distributed in small billabongs. After about two hours the fish would float unconscious to the surface. The sap from the inner bark was used as a bush antiseptic for cuts and wounds. Shavings from the inner bark were also soaked in water, and the resulting mixture sipped to relieve coughs and colds. The leaves were heated and wrapped around the head as a cure for headaches.

FISH POISON TREE

Acacia holosericea

THIS FISH POISON TREE GROWS extensively throughout northern Australia and is often found growing near watercourses. Although it can grow up to 4 m in height it is commonly seen as a rather spindly wattle of about 2 m. The tree can be distinguished by its curled, dried-up seed pods and grey-blue or silver leaves. The young leaves are extremely soft to touch.

USES The bark, leaves and green seed pods are crushed and washed in water to poison fish. This poisoning takes about half an hour to have an effect in a reasonably large pool of water. The fish would float to the surface, unconscious. They could be collected by hand and could be cooked and eaten in the usual manner. The water remains poisoned until further rains flush out the contaminated pools. The leaves and young green pods were sometimes lathered in water to use as a bush soap.

OTHER NAMES Soap wattle

FRESHWATER MANGROVE
Barringtonia acutangula

THE SAP FROM THIS TREE IS dangerous and can irritate the skin or burn the eyes. The freshwater mangrove can be found far inland, beside freshwater lagoons or river systems across the far north of Australia. Although it looks like a mangrove, it's not. It grows to about 5 m in height and produces leaves clustered in whorls at ends of branchlets. These leaves alternate along the central stem or branch. At various times during the year it produces bright red pendulous flowers with numerous stamens. The green fruits are inedible.

USES Aboriginal people used the roots, bark and leaves as a fish poison. These were pounded and washed in small waterways. The stunned fish rose to the water's surface and were caught by hand. The fish poison does affect the water for consumption. The poisoned water remains toxic and undrinkable until further rains flush out the polluted water.

OTHER NAMES River mangrove, itchy tree

GEEBUNG IS COMMONLY FOUND growing in open woodland country, particularly in sandy soils and well-drained country. This particular species is a straight slender tree, which can grow up to 5 m tall. The leaves are usually long and thin, and appear to droop from the tree. The trunk is dark coloured and deeply grooved. The small flowers are yellow or cream, with arched petals. From November to February small marble-sized fruit are produced. They ripen after falling to the ground, turning from green to yellowish green.

USES When ripe, the fruit is very sweet and can be eaten raw. The seed and skin of the fruit should not be eaten. Geebung fruit was a popular bush tucker. The bark and the leaves of the tree were also used by Aboriginal people as a medicine. An infusion was made to relieve sore throats and colds. A concoction of inner bark and water was used to bathe sore eyes.

OTHER NAMES Milky plum

GOBIN
Terminalia latipes

A RATHER SPINDLY TREE, PERHAPS reaching a height of up to 4 m and commonly found in open lowland forest. At the ends of the slim branches are bunches of oval-shaped leaves, which are yellowish-green in colour. During October to February clusters of fruit are produced. The small, teardrop-shaped fruit are initially green, but mature to a yellowish colour and fall to the ground, littering the floor underneath the tree.

USES Like many *Terminalia* species, the gobin fruit is extremely high in ascorbic acid (vitamin C). The skin and flesh of the fruit can be eaten raw. It has a slightly sweet–salty taste. The central stone was discarded. As a tucker, this fruit was a popular 'snack' food eaten when out walking or hunting.

OTHER NAMES Salty plum

GOLDEN GREVILLEA
Grevillea pteridifolia

GOLDEN GREVILLEA IS MOST commonly found growing in low-land swampy areas, river flats and open woodland. The tree is slim and up to 7 m tall. The leaves are deeply divided and fern-like, and the silky white under-sides give the tree a silvery appearance, particularly on a windy day. During the winter months, this gre-villea produces masses of bright orange bottle-brush type flowers. The flowers are 10–20 cm long, and carry large quantities of nectar, making them a favourite of honey-eating birds and insects.

USES The nectar has a pleasant sweet taste and was collected by 'bumping' the flowers over a suit-able container. This was done early in the morning before the sun's heat and birds had dried up the sup-ply. A drink was made by dunking flowers into a container of water until it assumed a syrupy consis-tency. Aboriginal people, especially children, enjoy eating the flowers.

OTHER NAMES Golden parrot tree, fern-leafed grevillea, swamp grevillea

GRASS TREE
Xanthorrhoea spp.

THIS DISTINCTIVE 'TREE' GROWS IN sandy or stony ground and can be found in all Australian states. In the early summer the long woody stalks produce creamy coloured flowers. The trunk exudes globules of yellow, dark red or black resin, which is often found in piles on the ground at the base of the tree.

USES The flower is laden with sweet nectar and can be sucked or dunked in water to produce a sweet drink. The drooping blades of grass or leaves and the white base of the grass tree can also be eaten raw. The base has a slightly bitter taste and is fibrous in texture. The crisp crown of the trunk was traditionally split open and eaten, but this kills the tree. The wooden flower stalks were often used by Aboriginal people to manufacture hunting spears. Dead trunks sometimes contain edible white grubs. The resin is flammable and could be used to start a fire. Dead trunks provide excellent firewood and burn with an intense heat, even in extremely wet conditions.

OTHER NAMES Black boy

GREEN PLUM
Buchanania obovata

T R E E

THE GREEN PLUM IS MOST OFTEN found growing in tropical woodland country, or behind beach-front areas. The tree is slender, with large, broad, leathery leaves, with the upper and lower sides looking very similar. Sprays of tiny cream flowers appear before the fruit. During December to March the tree produces an abundant crop of very small yellowish-green fruit, each containing a large clinging seed.

USES The green plum was a favourite tucker and an important bush medicine. When it is ripe it is still green, but soft, and can be shaken from the tree. It has a sour but pleasant taste. The roots were sometimes roasted and eaten, if food was short. The stems provided an effective toothache remedy. Stems were stripped of their bark and the inner wood quickly heated over a fire. The exuding sap was then applied directly to an aching tooth. Aboriginal people also used a hot poultice of leaves to help open wounds to heal, and an infusion was made into an eyewash.

OTHER NAMES Wild plum

GREY MANGROVE
Avicennia marina

THE GREY MANGROVE IS THE MOST widespread of the many mangrove species in Australia. It is commonly found on the outer edges or landward side of mangrove belts. The bushy tree is distinguished by its base, where pencil-like tips of the shallow root system protrude 10–20 cm from the mud. The bark is light grey. The leaves are small, green on top with a greyish–white velvety underside. The small, green, velvety seed pods are produced at any time of the year, and each contains a single seed.

USES The seeds are poisonous. In tropical areas Aboriginal people traditionally ate the starchy seeds after extensive preparation, which included steaming, washing and baking or boiling several times. The ash from the burnt wood of the grey mangrove was used to treat scabies, sores, cuts and other skin ailments.

OTHER NAMES White mangrove

THE GUAVA IS AN INTRODUCED tree, but is now widely distributed in eastern Australia. It can often be found growing beside creek lines or near water. The tree grows to about 4 m high, has a smooth bark and dark green leaves. The leaves have a number of deep and distinctive veins. From April to July the tree produces a large number of yellow-coloured fruit. These fruit can be as large as a tennis ball in size and are particularly favoured by birds. The fruit give off a distinct and strong aroma.

USES The pink-coloured flesh is edible raw. The hard circular seeds throughout the flesh can be swallowed or discarded.

GULF PLUM
Terminalia carpentariae

THE GULF PLUM CAN OFTEN BE found on coastal plains and hills around the Gulf of Carpentaria and the Top End. It commonly grows on sandstone or sandy flats, but can occur on stony ground. This tree can grow to 15 m but is usually smaller. The bark is grey. The large, broad leaves are dull green and typically crowded towards the ends of the branches. They turn a reddish colour before falling during the dry season. During September and October, when the tree is without leaves or commencing new growth, small (2–3 cm long) yellow–green fruits with a furry skin are produced. A thin layer of edible flesh surrounds a central stone.

USES The plums can be eaten raw. The taste is sour, but becomes agreeable after a few. Like other *Terminalia* species, the gulf plum contains very high levels of ascorbic acid (vitamin C). Aboriginal people also ate the clear gum which is exuded from the tree.

OTHER NAMES Wild peach

JOHNSON SATIN ASH
Syzygium johnsonii

THIS LARGE TROPICAL RAINFOREST tree, one of about fifty *Syzygium* species on Cape York, is endemic to eastern Queensland. The tree grows to around 8 m and has dark green, oval-shaped leaves. When the bark is cut it produces a deep red fibrous blaze. During the months of July, August and September the tree produces small, bright purple to whitish-coloured fruit. The fruit is generally first seen littering the forest floor. The 'cherries' have a very dry taste, typical of many native bush fruits, and a distinct blossom-like aroma.

USES The crisp white flesh and purple skin of the fruit are eaten raw. The large central seed is discarded.

JOHNSON RIVER ALMOND
Elaeocarpus bancroftii

AN IMPRESSIVE TROPICAL rainforest tree, growing up to 25 m. The tree has a spreading canopy of glossy green leaves that turn scarlet when they get older. During October, November and December it produces green, circular or oval-shaped pods. After falling to the forest floor, the pods rot away, revealing an extremely hard nut. The nut has four or five flattish sides, and is lightly pitted and tapered toward one end. An edible kernel is located inside the nut. The nuts can often be seen littering the forest floor for up to six months after podding, or found lodged with flood debris along rivers or creeks.

USES The kernel, which can be eaten raw, has a pleasant and distinctive taste, similar to coconut. Occasionally, some specimens produce two kernels.

OTHER NAMES Queensland almond

THIS TREE PREFERS A SANDY SOIL environment within the tropical woodland areas of northern Australia. The tree looks rather spindly and fairly sparse, even though it can grow to 7 m or more in height. Large oval leaves turn from green to yellow before falling to the ground during the cooler months. The fruiting season is at the end of the Wet, from March until June. The tear-shaped fruit turn from a rich green to a yellowish green when fully ripe. Ripe fruit found littering the ground are often tinged pink or red. Each plum has a central stone, which is surrounded by stringy, moist flesh.

USES This species of plum is the highest-known source of natural vitamin C in the world. One plum provides more vitamin C than six or eight oranges. The skin and flesh can be eaten raw. They have a pleasant, acidic taste, although in some specimens the taste is distinctly salty.

OTHER NAMES Salty plum, billy goat plum

KALUMBURU ALMOND
Terminalia cunninghamii

THE KALUMBURU ALMOND OCCURS in isolated pockets in north-western Australia within 100 km of the coast. It grows on sandy soils, usually in close proximity to sandstone outcrops. The tree grows to 8 m high, and older trees have a stunted appearance. The bark is grey and deeply grooved. The leaves are dull green and variable in size. The 'nuts' are this tree's most distinctive feature. They are found on the ground beneath the tree, and are most easily seen during the dry season after fires. These nuts are the size and shape of a walnut – outside they look just like a walnut – and are formed when the scanty flesh layer disappears after the fruit has fallen to the ground.

USES The 'nut' consists of a thick corky wood surrounding the kernel. This casing is broken away by sharp blows with a rock or hatchet. The kernel tastes like a commercial almond and is eaten raw.

THE KURRAJONG IS FOUND IN OPEN forest areas and coastal sandflat locations. This species is spindly in appearance and rarely grows taller than 3 m. The very large tri-lobed leaves are greenish-yellow, and appear as if eaten by insects. The red flowers are eye-catching. However, the woody boat-shaped seed pods, which appear from March to May, are the tree's most distinctive feature. They split open to reveal rows of seeds, which are yellow when fully ripe. The inside of the pod and the seeds are covered by felt-like hairs. These hairs are dangerous and should be kept well away from the eyes, nose and mouth.

USES The seeds were an excellent source of nutrition but great care was required in preparing them. When mature, the pods were roasted over a fire to singe the hairs, then the hairs were removed. The roasted seeds have a pleasant nutty flavour. Aboriginal people also used the wood to make fire sticks and the bark fibre to make string and rope.

OTHER NAMES Red kurrajong

LADY APPLE
Syzygium suborbiculare

THE NATIVE OR LADY APPLE TREE IS often found in sandy soils in tropical woodland locations across the Cape York region and the Top End of northern Australia. It is usually a large solid broad-leafed tree, growing up to 12 m. The leathery leaves are almost circular and positioned opposite each other along the branch. During October to February the tree produces clusters of white, tasselled flowers. The fruits are a red–pinkish colour when ripe, roughly oval in shape, and often appear to have been penetrated by grubs or insects.

USES The apples, eaten raw, have a crisp texture and slightly acidic taste. The seeds of the fruit should not be eaten even though they are not known to be harmful. The lady apple tree was also a source of bush medicine. The leaves were heated and applied to wounds to stop bleeding. The bark and leaves were made into an infusion for diarrhoea.

OTHER NAMES Native apple, red bush apple

LEICHHARDT TREE
Nauclea orientalis

TREE

A LARGE SOLID TREE FOUND IN THE open woodland and closed tropical woodland areas of northern Australia. The tree is only found beside watercourses such as creek lines and rivers and so is a good indicator of fresh water. The tree has large oval-shaped glossy green leaves, with branches that tend to grow horizontally. The distinctive yellow flowers resemble a spiky round ball. From November to April, the edible fruit, which looks like a dirty golf ball, can be seen. Not all fruit are perfectly circular in shape.

USES The fruit, eaten raw, has a slightly bitter taste. The flesh and the small black seeds under the skin are eaten, the skin being discarded. The bark, roots and leaves of the tree were pulverised and thrown in pools of water to stupefy fish. After floundering to the water's surface, stunned, the fish could be easily caught, then cooked and eaten.

OTHER NAMES Leichhardt pine

LITTLE GOOSEBERRY TREE
Buchanania arborescens

THIS TREE IS FOUND IN TROPICAL woodland areas bordering watercourses. It is related to the mango, to which it bears a close resemblance, except for the fruit. It grows to about 10 m in height and has alternate, leathery leaves, up to 20 cm long, with distinctive yellowish veins. Sprays of tiny, white, fragrant flowers are followed by small, green fruit towards the end of the wet season. The edible fruit are around 1 cm in diameter, and turn purplish when ripe.

USES Eaten raw, the plums are sweet and pulpy with a thin rind, not unlike a gooseberry. The unripe fruits can be boiled in water to produce an agreeable acid-tasting drink. Aboriginal people used the inner bark to prepare an infusion for use as an eyewash and to bathe cuts or wounds.

OTHER NAMES Green plum

ALTHOUGH NOT A NATIVE SPECIES, the mango now inhabits rainforest fringes and creek lines in the tropics, and is a common sight around abandoned dwellings and stockyards. The tree has a large spreading crown of dark green leathery leaves, and grows up to 10 m high. The bark of the thick trunk is rough and grey. Early each wet season the fruit is produced in large numbers. Mangoes are large, up to 15 cm long, and rounded with a distinct groove running down one side to a small, curved end. Young fruit are green, but ripen to pink, orange or yellow with a powdery appearance on the skin. Ripe fruit may be rare if flying foxes are prevalent – the sound of squabbling flying foxes at night often indicates a nearby mango tree.

USES The skin should be peeled off. The flesh is orange, usually stringy, and clings to the large central seed. The flavour is pleasantly sweet, but sometimes has a turpentine taste. The tree's sap can burn the skin if not washed off immediately.

NATIVE APPLE
Syzygium eucalyptoides

THE NATIVE APPLE TREE IS USUALLY found growing on sandy or gravel-like soils in creek lines across the very top of northern Australia. It reaches a height of around 5 m and has slender, weeping branches. The leaves are slender, grey-green and resemble gum leaves. From August to November, dense clusters of white flowers, similar to gum-tree flowers, appear. Edible fruit is usually produced during August, September and October.

USES The small pink-cream fruit of the native apple is eaten raw and has a tangy, but dry taste. Aboriginal people used the native apple as a bush medicine. The inner reddish bark was mashed and mixed with water and the resulting concoction applied as a wash to the entire body for the relief of general sickness. The body wash must not be drunk.

OTHER NAMES Bush apple

THE NATIVE POMEGRANATE TREE IS a rainforest species but it can be quite often found in dry tropical woodland country as well. It can grow to a height of 6 m, however it is commonly much shorter than that. The bark is deeply ribbed and sharp spikes are recessed into the cavities. The leaves of the tree are oval in shape and the small, white flowers are quite fragile. During September, October and November, the tree produces an edible fruit that can grow to about the size of a tennis ball, depending on the growth cycle.

USES When fully ripe, the fruit turn from green to yellow and have a rough, almost warty appearance. The flesh inside is edible raw, however the large seeds embedded in the flesh are discarded.

NONDA PLUM
Parinari nonda

TREE

THE NONDA PLUM TREE TENDS TO favour dry sandy soils and can be seen growing in tropical woodland areas. The tree itself is reasonably solid but only reaches a height of about 8 m. The branches have a drooping, pendulous appearance particularly during August to November when it produces masses of orange–brown, oval-shaped fruit. The leaves are often dark green on the upper surface and light green on the underside.

USES The flesh of the fruit, which is edible raw, has a dry mealy taste and texture. A large ribbed stone or seed is found in each plum. The fruit tends to ripen after falling to the ground. Aboriginal people would sometimes bury the fruit from a few days to a week, during which time it would ripen. This was also a way of storing the fruit for longer periods. The floury pulp of the fruit can be ground and baked into a kind of damper.

 THIS IS A MEDIUM–SIZED TREE OF the tropical rainforest and closed tropical woodland areas. It is most often found beside watercourses such as rivers and streams. When the trunk of the tree is cut, a bright red watery sap exudes from the trunk. The tree has large tapered fleshy leaves that are green on top, silver-coloured on the underside. From June to September the tree produces numerous rusty brown capsules, which have a felt-like texture. When mature the capsules split open to reveal a red- to brown-coloured kernel. This kernel is covered with a bright red netting.

USES The kernel is ground to produce the spice 'nutmeg'. The ground kernel has a distinct nutmeg taste. The red netting or 'mace' is also edible and requires no preparation. The trunk of the tree was used by Aboriginal people for the construction of dug-out canoes.

OTHER NAMES Native nutmeg

ONION WOOD
Syzygium sp.

A TROPICAL RAINFOREST TREE THAT can reach up to 30 m in height, which appears to favour high rainfall areas below 800 m in altitude. The flaky-textured bark of the tree may be whitish-grey or orange–pink in colour. The leaves are slightly oval in shape. During July, August and September the tree produces large pink–red fruit, squarish in shape and containing one central large seed. The fruit is produced in large clusters, which tend to droop or hang from the tree. This is one of many *Syzygium* species that grow on Cape York Peninsula.

USES The crisp flesh and skin of the fruit, which is eaten raw, has a slightly tangy taste. The fruit usually has a high water content and is not particularly nutritious, but would have provided variety in the traditional bush tucker diet.

PACIFIC ROSEWOOD
Thespesia populneoides

THIS SMALL TREE IS FOUND IN SMALL pockets across the top end of Queensland and the Northern Territory and in The Kimberley. It grows in sandy loam-type soils, always in close proximity to the sea. The Pacific rosewood tree has a similar appearance to the **cotton tree** (*Hibiscus tiliaceus*), sometimes called the beach-growing hibiscus. Leaves are large, heart-shaped and a rather dull green in colour. The tree also produces small smooth woody capsules. At various times throughout the year showy yellow flowers with a maroon centre are produced.

USES The flowers as well as the young leaves and buds of the tree can be eaten raw or cooked. The wood was sometimes used for fire sticks and spears.

OTHER NAMES Indian tulip tree

PANDANUS

Pandanus spp.

TREE

DIFFERENT PANDANUS SPECIES CAN be found growing across northern Australia. The trees can grow to around 10 m, and have elongated ribbon-like leaves, often arranged in a spiral fashion. The rather stiff leaves have a succession of sharp, recurved teeth running along either edge and the leaf's central spine. The giant fruit is similar in appearance to a pineapple. These fruit ripen to yellow then bright orange from August to January. Each fruit is composed of a number of wedge-shaped segments, attached to a central core. Each segment contains up to six almond-like nuts.

USES The nuts have an excellent nutritional content and are delicious raw or roasted, but difficult to extract. The fleshy orange pulp in the wedges of some species had to be treated before being eaten. The terminal bud was sometimes eaten raw. The white inner portion of the prop roots, or stilt roots, was used as a bush medicine. The leaves were used to make mats, shelters, baskets and so on.

OTHER NAMES Screw pine

THIS IMPRESSIVE TALL TREE, WHICH can grow to 30 m high, is found growing in heavy soil and in close proximity to fresh water, usually beside a creek or river system, near billabongs or seasonally flooded areas. The papery bark can be cream or grey in colour. The smooth flat leaves droop, creating a weeping appearance. During June and July the tree becomes heavily laden with cream-coloured blossom. At that time, fragrance from the nectar has a caramel aroma.

USES Aboriginal people, especially children, would suck nectar from the flowers, eat the flowers raw, or dunk them in water to produce a sweet drink. During the flowering period, the tree is popular with **native bees** (*Trigona* spp.). The leaves were also chewed and sucked, or inhaled for the relief of head colds and flu, and had an effect similar to eucalyptus oil. The bark was widely used: to wrap food for cooking, as an instant food container, and to make shelters, to name just a few uses.

OTHER NAMES Tea-tree, melaleuca

PEANUT TREE
Sterculia quadrifida

THIS TREE IS FOUND IN A VARIETY of environments throughout northern and eastern Australia, most often in coastal regions. It tends to grow in well-drained sandy soils. The tree can reach over 15 m in height and is often deciduous, giving it a sparse appearance. Flowers are small and greenish-yellow. From August to December it produces attractive red–orange seed pods which split open to reveal a similar-coloured lining. Attached to this lining are a number of jet-black seeds, about the size and shape of a peanut kernel.

USES The creamy white centre of these seeds can be eaten raw and has a pleasant peanut-like taste. The broad green leaves were used by Aboriginal people as a bush medicine. The leaves were crushed and applied to open wounds and sores. The inner bark was boiled and the liquid used to bathe infected eyes. The fibre of the inner bark was also used to make twine or string.

OTHER NAMES Monkey nut tree

THE PLUMWOOD IS FOUND IN THE top of the Northern Territory and Kimberley regions. A slender upright tree, growing to 15 m, it is usually found in association with gum trees along creek lines or on black soil plains. The small, very narrow leaves fall from the tree by the end of July. Flowers are cream to green with numerous stamens. The smooth-skinned fruit, produced during the wet season, fall to the ground from March to May. They are purple when ripe. These fruits consist of a thin, fleshy rind around a large central stone or 'nut'. The nut is thick and woody, and to be opened must be cracked by sharp blows with a rock or hatchet. This nut is easily found beneath the trees during the dry season, particularly after fires.

USES The nut contains an edible kernel resembling a small plump almond; the taste is similar to commercial almonds. Aboriginal people used the timber to make woomeras, and also as fire sticks and digging sticks.

QUANDONG
Santalum lanceolatum

THE QUANDONG TREE IS A PLANT OF the arid regions and dry open savannah, but can also be found on flat ground beside inland waterways. It has the appearance of a tall bush, growing to around 3 m high. The tree has a drooping eucalyptus-like growth with green to grey leaves. Edible fruit are produced during summer and autumn. The green unripe fruits resemble gumnuts in appearance, changing to bright red then almost black when ripe. The black–red edible flesh surrounds a large central stone, and may stain the fingers and mouth.

USES The berries were eaten raw and were considered good tucker. They are succulent with a very sweet flavour. As a medicine, the central seeds were ground up, mixed with water, and applied to skin sores. The plant was also used for other medicinal purposes.

OTHER NAMES Wild plum, bush plum

TREE

THIS SANDPAPER FIG IS MOST OFTEN found in open areas or around the verges of rainforest. The tree grows to a height of around 3 m, and has broad dark green leaves with a rough upper surface. At various times throughout the year the tree produces numbers of figs. These figs are slightly larger than a marble and turn blackish–purple in colour and quite soft when mature. They have a slightly furry surface. When ripe they are particularly popular with birds.

USES The entire fig can be eaten raw and has an excellent flavour. When picked from the tree, a small white dot of sap may appear on the base of the fig. This should be wiped off before eating. The leaves are extremely rough to touch and were used by Aboriginal people as a very effective 'sandpaper'.

OTHER NAMES Purple fig, creek fig

SHE-OAK
Casuarina equisetifolia

THIS SPECIES OF *Casuarina* TENDS to occur mostly in coastal sand-dune country across northern Queensland and the Northern Territory. Other related species are distributed throughout Australia. A tall, graceful tree, which can grow to 30 m, it has a somewhat pendulous look with its drooping, needle-thin branchlets. Small woody 'oak apples' appear in early summer.

USES The wispy leaves and in some cases the young green oak apples were chewed by Aboriginal people as a thirst-quencher. The fruits have an extremely acidic taste and contain an acid similar to citric acid. This activates the salivary glands, thereby relieving the symptoms of thirst. In some species of *Casuarina*, the roots have been known to yield viable quantities of water. A traditional bush medicine was an infusion made from the inner bark and used as a mouthwash to relieve sore throats and toothaches. The mixture was not swallowed.

OTHER NAMES Coast she-oak, whistling tree

SILK COTTON TREE
Bombax ceiba

THIS LARGE, STOUT TREE CAN BE found in pockets of the Cape York region, and the very top of the Northern Territory. The tree prefers moist but well-drained soils or the dry edges of watercourses such as creeks and rivers. It can grow to 20 m, dominating the surrounding vegetation. The erect trunk is very distinctive, being covered in a mass of cone-shaped prickles. During July, August and September the tree produces masses of elegant bright red or orange flowers. The flowers soon begin to drop from the tree, littering the ground. The elongated seed pods contain a mass of silk-like fibre or 'kapok'.

USES Aboriginal people would roast the edible tap root of young plants. The wood of the tree trunk is very soft and was a favourite timber to make into canoes. The inner bark of the trunk was also made into a strong twine.

OTHER NAMES Bombax, kapok tree, canoe tree

SOAP TREE
Alphitonia excelsa

THE SMALL SOAP TREE GROWS IN closed tropical savannah and is particularly common along creek lines. The bark is smooth and grey. The distinctive leaves are a rich green on the upper surface, but silvery grey-white underneath. Flowers are very small, sweet-scented and cream–green. The tree produces masses of red to black berries, each having a distinct raised rib around its circumference. The berries split open to reveal a red centre and reddish seed.

USES The soap tree was commonly used as a fish poison. The berries and leaves are crushed and floated out in a pool of water. The plant contains saponin, which removes oxygen from the water, causing the fish to flounder to the surface. However, fish poisoning renders the water undrinkable and was usually done toward the end of the dry season, or in an emergency. The leaves, if rubbed vigorously, lather somewhat like soap and can be used as such.

OTHER NAMES Shampoo tree

TREE

THE STRYCHNINE TREE IS COMMONLY found throughout northern Australia. This bushy tree grows to a height of up to 5 m, and has dark green, oval-shaped leaves. From February to August, masses of attractive orange fruit are produced. These fruit, which look like miniature oranges, are not edible. The fruit is poisonous. The seeds of the fruit contain strychnine.

USES Aboriginal people mashed up the fruit, the bark of the tree and the leaves and used the resulting compress as a body wash to help cure general illness. The same mixture was also used as a fish poison in small water catchments. It was thoroughly mixed with the water. The stunned fish soon floated to the surface and could be caught by hand and scooped onto the bank. They were then cooked and eaten in the usual fashion.

TAMARIND
Tamarindus indica

THE TAMARIND TREE WAS introduced by Macassan fishermen and traders who visited Australia's northern waters hundreds of years ago. It tends to be found near the coast, around abandoned homesteads and old mines, and along river banks downstream from such areas. The tamarind is very large, up to 25 m in height, with a thick trunk and dense canopy coming right down to the ground, or to a height grazed by stock. The leaves are feather-like. From June to October elongated brown pods hang from the tree. When ripe, the brittle outer shell can be cracked away to reveal a rusty coloured flesh surrounding shiny brown seeds.

USES This edible flesh is tart to taste. The flesh can also be soaked in water to make a refreshing drink. The flesh is rich in phosphorus and calcium and has a laxative effect if taken in quantity. Young plants, leaves and flowers of the tamarind tree can be cooked and eaten as greens.

TENNIS BALL FRUIT
Siphonodon pendulus

TREE

A FAIRLY ERECT TREE FOUND IN tropical woodland areas. The tree has a 'weeping willow' appearance with its drooping thin branches. Long thin leaves are positioned alternately along the branches. From December to February and June to October round fruits are produced. Initially the fruit is green in colour but turns to yellow when fully ripe. The skin of the fruit often has an eaten appearance, possibly caused by borers or grubs.

USES The dry flesh of the fruit, edible raw, has a slightly gritty texture and a sweet banana-like taste. Large seeds found in the flesh should be discarded. A decoction of the fruit, inner bark of the trunk and the roots was used as a poultice for broken bones, sprains and joint dislocations. The poultice was heated and rubbed or held in place on the injured area.

TREE FERN
Cyathea spp.

THESE LARGE TREE FERNS CAN BE found in tropical rainforest and moist eucalypt forest areas. They prefer moist ground but in association with sunlight. The ferns grow to over 5 m. The young fronds, before shooting, are curled rather like a snail's shell. These are called crosiers, or fiddle-heads, and are covered in brown hairs.

USES After removing the hairs, the curled fronds were eaten raw, although they do have a bitter taste. This taste can be removed by washing and cooking the fronds before eating. The bitterness is due to the presence of tannin. The soft pithy apex or terminal bud of the tree trunk is also edible and contains a large amount of starch. In some areas, Aboriginal people would wash the starchy pith and bake it. To eat the terminal bud, however, destroys the tree.

TROPICAL ALMOND
Terminalia catappa

THIS TREE IS FOUND IN TROPICAL coastal regions. It grows to a height of 20 m, with branches tending to grow horizontally. Very large oval-shaped leaves turn from dark green to red then purple in colour, and can be found littering the ground. From January to April the tree produces a number of pods. When they fall from the tree these pods are green to red in colour and tapered or pointed at both ends. Inside is a single elongated 'almond'. The casing consists of a 'corky' fibrous material. The nuts can be opened by striking at one of the pointed ends with a heavy object. This should split the casing in two, revealing the kernel.

USES The almonds, which can be eaten raw, have a crisp texture, a nutty flavour and contain a high proportion of edible oil. The smooth skin of the casing is particularly favoured by ground rodents and sand crabs.

OTHER NAMES Sea almond, Indian almond

WHITE ASPEN
Acronychia acronychioides

WHITE ASPEN TREES ARE FOUND IN upland and lowland areas and are closely associated with tropical rainforest areas. These trees are small to medium in height, usually growing to about 15 m. The attractive rich green leaves have a smooth oily texture. These leaves feature a distinctive central mid-rib and light veins running to the edges of the leaf. Tiny white flowers are followed from July to October by masses of yellowish-coloured globular fruit. Although small, only about 1.5 cm in diameter, each fruit contains a single large seed.

USES The skin and flesh surrounding this seed can be eaten raw and has a sweet-sour taste according to the degree of maturity.

WHITE WOOD
Atalaya varifolia

THE WHITE WOOD IS A SMALL TREE favouring sandy or loamy soils and found in dry open forest and sparse woodland country. The tree grows to about 5 m in height and fully grown trees are easily mistaken for white gums. The young saplings are quite different in appearance from the mature trees. Initially the young tree looks like a fern. These young trees are always found in close proximity to the larger parent trees. The saplings begin to appear after the first influence of the wet season, usually December and January.

USES When the tree was at a very juvenile stage, Aboriginal people would use the tap root for food. The root was dug up, washed clean, the outer bark scraped away, and the fibrous root eaten raw. Young roots have a pleasant sweetish taste while older specimens are far too fibrous to chew. These roots were also baked on hot coals.

WILD ORANGE
Capparis canescens

THIS WILD ORANGE TREE FAVOURS open forest country and the fringes of watercourses. A rather small, scruffy tree, it grows to a height of about 3 m. The oval-shaped leaves are dull blue to green in colour. During the wet season, round ball-like fruit are produced. The outer casing often has a gnarled appearance. The fruit itself is attached to the tree by a distinctive stalk structure. The smooth stalk leads from the fruit, does a 90° bend, and then has a largish, knobbly joint. From this joint, the fruit is attached to a twig or branch. Inside, the fruit is filled with a bright orange pulp and large hard seeds embedded in the pulp.

USES The yellow pulp of the fruit has a pleasant, sweet taste, not unlike fruit salad. The seeds are not eaten. These fruits were a popular bush tucker.

OTHER NAMES Native caper

WILD ORANGE
Capparis mitchellii

A SMALL, CITRUS-LIKE TREE THAT grows in dry, open savannah country. The wild orange reaches 3–5 m in height. The bark is rough and recurved hooks are present on the main branches and twigs, especially on the new growth. The leaves are a dull, dark green and unusual cream or white flowers precede the fruit. From November to February the tree produces lemon-shaped fruit which have a slightly furry skin. They turn from green to yellow, become soft and fragrant then drop to the ground. The tree is drought resistant and fire tolerant.

USES The fruits are filled with an orange-coloured pulp which is eaten raw, and has a very sweet taste with a slight flavour of mango. Embedded in the pulp are a number of rounded seeds that can be ingested but should be swallowed whole, not chewed. These fruit are still a favourite bush tucker today.

OTHER NAMES Native pomegranate

WONGI PLUM
Manilkara kauki

THE WONGI PLUM IS FOUND IN coastal regions of the Torres Strait and Cape York area. The trees grow to about 6 m in height and from a distance have a distinct silvery appearance. This is due to the leathery oval–shaped leaves being white or silver on the underside. The fruit appears from July to September, with some seasonal variation. When fully mature, the elongated fruit has an orange to red or wine colouring. Each fruit has a longish stem attached to it, and one or two long seeds inside the flesh.

USES Ripe plums can be eaten raw and have a sweet taste. The fruit is very popular with Torres Strait pigeons as well as the fruit bats. Aboriginal people would sometimes bury the fruits, to hasten the ripening process.

BITTER YAM
Amorphophallus spp.

VINE

THIS YAM IS POISONOUS. IT IS MOST often found growing near freshwater streams in low coastal country, in particular coastal monsoon vine thickets. The plant has one central stem or trunk and an umbrella of dark green leaves radiating from the top. All the leaves are deeply 'split' or divided. The central stem grows from a large underground tuber.

USES The yam is poisonous but was eaten by Aboriginal people after very extensive treatment. This would involve slicing the tuber, then washing it in running fresh water. The slices would be left to sit in a running stream for no less than two days, after which the flesh would be mulched into a cake and baked on hot coals. Even then, only a small portion was usually eaten. The juice or moisture from the tuber had to be kept well away from the eyes and mouth.

BUSH BANANA

Marsdenia australis

THE BUSH BANANA IS WIDELY distributed throughout the country, particularly in the drier regions. Often the vine can be found growing beside seemingly dry creek beds and watercourses in the arid zone, because of underground moisture. The fruit grows on a vine that climbs up small bushes and shrubs. The long slender leaves grow opposite each other along the vine's stem. Like most arid-zone plants it relies heavily on rainfall to reproduce, and consequently fruiting occurs following rain, especially from November to April. The fruit has a moisture content of over 70 per cent.

USES The thick green casing of the young fruit can be eaten raw and tastes similar to fresh green peas. Inside the casing there are flattish seeds with strands of white whiskers, which assist with the wind dispersal. The vine's flowers can be sucked for nectar and eaten raw. Aboriginal people also sometimes cook the banana in hot ashes.

OTHER NAMES Native pear

VINE

 A SCRAMBLING VINE, COMMON IN northern Australia, which inhabits open woodland, closed tropical woodland, and sunlit areas of the tropical rainforest. In general, it appears to favour a humid tropical environment. The plant is originally from South America. Tasselled white flowers, with a dark purple throat or centre, are similar to domestic passionfruit. The leaves have three distinct lobes, again similar to the common passionfruit. Throughout the year the vine produces small fruits, about the size and shape of a marble, that turn from green to yellow when fully ripe. The fruit is encased in a fragile 'net' that eventually dries up and falls away.

USES The fruit contains a number of black seeds embedded in a grey, pulpy membrane, all of which can be eaten raw. They have a sweet, tangy taste. The thin papery skin is discarded. Green fruit are toxic – do not eat.

OTHER NAMES Love-in-the-mist, stinking passionfruit, wild passionfruit

BUSH POTATO
Brachystelma glabriflorum

THESE PLANTS SEEM TO FAVOUR sandy soils, particularly in coastal environs. The plant looks like a piece of grass, however the main stem, which grows to around 30 cm high, is stronger and thicker than grass. Within about 50 cm of the surface there is a round or oblong-shaped tuber, which looks and tastes like a potato. The plants are most easily found immediately after the wet season, but can usually be found all year, unless bush fires have been through the area.

USES The tuber was eaten raw or cooked. Some specimens have a slightly nutty flavour.

THE CAPE GOOSEBERRY, FOUND IN coastal beach areas and rainforest verges in northern Australia, is an introduced species. It is a low scrambling plant, growing to less than a metre tall, with dull greyish to dark green leaves. The leaves are covered in very fine hairs. (*Physalis minima*, a related native species, has soft, smooth leaves.) The fruit, a favourite with birds, is produced throughout the year. The round green fruit is encased in a papery capsule. As the fruit matures it turns yellowish, and the capsule becomes brown and brittle. The fruit is filled with masses of minute seeds.

USES Aboriginal people ate the entire fruit raw. Early settlers also ate some gooseberry species. The fruit has a pleasant, sweet to sour taste depending on the degree of maturity or ripeness.

OTHER NAMES Native gooseberry

A SCRAMBLING VINE FOUND ACROSS northern Australia in a range of habitats including rainforest, tropical woodland and arid areas. The bush does not have leaves, but produces a mass of green, pencil-thick, succulent branches. Small white flowers appear from late winter to spring. When broken, the branches exude a white sap.

USES The sap was used by Aboriginal people as a bush medicine. It was applied with some success to stop wounds bleeding, and help cure sores and skin rashes. The white sap is corrosive – keep well away from the mouth and eyes.

OTHER NAMES Caustic bush, milk bush, snake vine

THIS LOW GROUND CREEPER SOME-times grows as a small branching shrub. It is usually found in savannah woodland country and wetland areas. The leaves range from broadly heart-shaped to distinctly five-lobed, and have serrated edges. The stems and flower stalks are covered with hairs. The attractive flowers measure up to 13 cm across, and may be watermelon pink or yellow or even white in colour, with a dark red throat. The plant begins its annual growth with the first rains of the wet season, and dies back early in winter. A small edible tuber, resembling a white carrot, can usually be found 6–10 cm below the ground.

USES The tuber can easily be dug up and eaten raw or cooked. It has a pleasant carrot-like taste. The young leaves and shoots of the plant are also edible.

OTHER NAMES Climbing hibiscus, bush carrot

DESERT YAM
Ipomoea costata

THE DESERT YAM GROWS IN SANDY soil in Australia's arid zone. It usually appears just after rainfall, with its lush, rich green foliage standing out against the sandy countryside. It is often found scrambling or climbing around dead trees or bushes. It produces a pink, trumpet-shaped flower, and has distinctly heart-shaped leaves. The root system, which has edible underground bulbs, spreads out in all directions from the central stem. The bulbs are usually located about half a metre underground with each plant capable of producing several bulbs. As the bulbs increase in size, they often cause the ground surface above to crack very slightly. Aboriginal women would locate the hairline crack in the ground, up to a metre from the main stem, as this would indicate just where to dig for the bulbs.

USES Yams or bush potatoes were an important staple food for Aboriginal people. The starchy tubers were usually roasted.

OTHER NAMES Bush potato

A PARASITIC, LEAFLESS VINE, sometimes found in tropical forest country, but particularly favouring sandy soils and beach-front areas. The vine is wire-thin, green through bright yellow to orange in colour, and tangles itself along the ground and over low shrubs and trees. It sometimes forms a dense mat of entanglement over surrounding ground and vegetation. The vine produces small green berries, slightly smaller than a pea, which turn translucent-white when fully ripe. Each of the berries has a single seed. The berries are found on the vines throughout the year.

USES The berries were sometimes eaten raw, but only in small quantities. The seeds were discarded. Although sweet, they contain small quantities of poisonous alkaloids, which in large doses can bring on stomach cramps, or may even prove fatal. The juice extracted from the crushed vines was used as a bush medicine, applied directly to ulcers and lacerations.

OTHER NAMES Dodder laurel, devil's twine

GIDGEE GIDGEE
Abrus precatorius

THIS CLIMBING VINE CAN BE FOUND throughout the northern and eastern regions of Australia. It has fine feather-like foliage. The vine scrambles over low vegetation and produces a cluster of small pods, like pea pods. When the pod turns brown and splits open, it reveals the shiny red seeds with a black spot. The brightly coloured red-and-black seeds of the gidgee gidgee are extremely poisonous. One seed, crushed and swallowed, is enough to kill a person. These seeds contain the poison abrin. If particles from the seeds, or sap from the bark, come into contact with cuts or scratches, they can cause poisoning, with possibly fatal results.

USES Aboriginal people used the vine as a fish poison. It would be pounded and washed in small pools of water to stun or kill fish. The fish could then be cooked and eaten in the normal manner. Sometimes the seeds were used for decorative purposes.

OTHER NAMES Crabs eye, rosary pea

THIS SCRAMBLING VINE IS COMMON in many beach areas of Australia. It is invariably found covering the tops of coastal sand dunes, and is made conspicuous by its attractive purple or mauve bell-shaped flowers. The plant gets its common name from the shape of the leaves, which have one lobe on either side of the central vein or midrib. The leaves are thick and shiny.

USES The plant is poisonous and was only eaten after lengthy preparation. The bark would be removed from the central tap root, the root washed and then the fleshy portion boiled. The leaves of the vine were used by Aboriginal people as bush medicine, to relieve stings and bites from insects, stingray and snakes. The leaves would be heated on hot rocks and then applied as a poultice to the affected area. In this manner, the leaves are also reportedly a cure for skin irritations, boils, skin infections, ringworm and haemorrhoids.

OTHER NAMES Convolvulus, morning glory

Gulaka
Vigna radiata

 This climbing vine is often found scrambling over shrubs or fallen timber in closed tropical savannah country. It has bright green heart-shaped leaves, tiny greenish-yellow flowers and long green seed pods. It usually dies during the dry season, but between February and May can be found with new growth springing up from an underground tuber.

USES Although the seeds, seed sprouts and sometimes the seed pods are eaten in Asia, Aboriginal people used the underground tuber as a food resource. When dug up it looks like a long white parsnip. The tuber was eaten either raw or cooked, and has a sweet-potato taste with a high moisture content.

OTHER NAMES Wild mung bean, finger bean

VINE

A VIGOROUS CLIMBING VINE FOUND in rainforest areas and moist gullies, and particularly common where the rainforest comes right down to the coastal dunes. It sometimes forms a high canopy over the tops of tall trees. Shiny, leathery leaves grow in groups of three on short opposite stems arising from the main vine. It produces clusters of sparse, greenish–white flowers.

USES The vine is used as a bush medicine to cure the symptoms of headache, head colds and sinus. Leaves are crushed and cupped in the clasped hands to capture the aroma. The hands are then placed to the nose and the pungent aroma inhaled. A sharp piercing sensation is felt along the nasal passages. Sap from the headache vine contains an irritant, so people with sensitive skin should wash their hands as soon as possible.

OTHER NAMES Traveller's vine

KALUMBURU YAM

Ipomoea sp.

THE KALUMBURU YAM APPEARS TO have a fairly small distribution, centred around the Kalumburu area of The Kimberley. It grows in a coastal environment and particularly favours sandy soil behind the beach line, in open woodland country. The vine, with its heart-shaped leaves, can often be seen growing around the base of other bushes and shrubs. It has trumpet-shaped flowers and green leaves, frequently with a yellow tinge around the edges. Vines are most easily seen during the dry season, from around May until November.

USES The large, lumpy yarns are edible. The traditional method of cooking was to roast the yam on hot coals. When washed, skinned, sliced and then thoroughly boiled, they have a taste very similar to boiled potato.

OTHER NAMES Bush potato

A PROLIFIC, PRICKLY CLIMBING VINE with palm-like fronds, found in the tropical rainforest. It produces lengths of yellow, jointed cane up to 150 m long. Edible berries grow near the climbing end of the vine from November to February. These berries have a scale-like skin and a large seed surrounded by a thin layer of flesh.

USES The berries, eaten raw, have a slightly sour taste. The long, flexible thongs of the vine, with their recurved 'wait-a-while' hooks, were used to snag **freshwater prawns** (*Macrobrachium australiense*), and extract **witchetty grubs** (*Cossidae* sp.) from rotting logs and tree trunks. Many species of the vine store considerable drinkable water, particularly in the ground-looping sections. To obtain this water, the cane would be cut into short sections, held upright and drained. The cane itself could be used for constructing fish or animal traps. The palm-like fronds, reputedly discourage leeches when scattered around sleeping areas.

OTHER NAMES Wait-a-while

LONG YAM
Dioscorea transversa

THE LONG YAM IS FOUND IN tropical rainforest and closed tropical woodland regions. The climbing vine has broad, rich green, heart-shaped leaves with veins all originating from the leaf stem point. The distinctive seed pod has three fine wings, all joined along a central axis or stem. The individual wings are semi-circular to oval in shape. The wire-like vine leads to an underground tuber or 'yam'. These 'yams' are usually located well below ground level and can grow to considerable lengths. Their seasonal period depends on the preceding rain or wet season. The yam is elongated, whitish-brown, with a fine hairy root system on the outer surface.

USES Long yams were a staple food in northern coastal areas – finding and digging for them was an important skill. These yams can be eaten raw, although they were usually roasted. They have a definite potato-like flavour.

OTHER NAMES Pencil yam

MALOGA BEAN
Vigna lanceolata

VINE

A VERY THIN, TWINING VINE OF both the woodland and rainforest-margin areas. The vine, similar in appearance to the domestic 'bean', attaches its climbing tendrils to other plants and shrubs. The vine is easily identified by its tapered trifoliate leaf structure. Leaves are narrow with a prominent central mid-rib. From February to July, small pea-like flowers appear. These flowers are often yellow, but occasionally blue. The flowers are followed by a thick, rounded edible pod.

USES The long parsnip-shaped roots were a staple food for inland Aboriginal tribes, being available all year. The starchy root was usually roasted and has a potato-like taste. The green pods were eaten raw.

OTHER NAMES Yellow-flowering bean, pencil yam

MATCHBOX BEAN
Entada phaseoloides

A ROBUST CLIMBING VINE OF THE tropical regions, particularly the east coast of Cape York. The vine favours the tree canopy of creek lines and watercourses. Climbing to the upper forest canopy, the vine produces giant hanging bean pods, scalloped in shape and a metre or more in length. The pods, which become quite woody on drying out, contain a number of round, somewhat flat, shiny brown beans. The beans are quite large. The pods often wash up along the coast.

USES The beans are poisonous, but were traditionally eaten after extensive preparation. The inner white section of the beans was first extracted and baked, then pounded to form a sort of flour, then soaked in fresh water. The resulting 'porridge' was eaten without further treatment. It is still rather bland and tasteless. The bark and stem of the vine were soaked in water, crushed, and the resulting lather used as a soap. This lather is toxic and contains saponin, so it was also used as a fish poison.

OTHER NAMES Queensland bean

NATIVE GRAPE

Ampelocissus acetosa

THIS VINE GROWS IN PARTS OF northern Australia and is common in Arnhem Land and Cape York. It is often seen in sunlit areas towards the end of the wet season. The vine may be freestanding, or clamber over fallen logs and up branches of surrounding vegetation. The largish leaves appear in groups of two or three. During February to May small clusters of 6–12 grapes are produced. Initially the fleshy fruit are green but turn a very dark purple when fully mature.

USES The fruit can be eaten raw and at first provides a pleasant, sweet taste. Within a minute or so, however, the throat will suffer a slight burning sensation. This reaction is harmless. Aboriginal people would sometimes roast the thick underground roots, but only after considerable preparation. Even after this preparation, the roots will still burn the mouth when chewed. The juice is said to have been used as an antidote for death adder and other snake bites.

OTHER NAMES Wild grape

NATIVE GRAPE
Cissus hypoglauca

THIS PARTICULAR NATIVE GRAPE IS most often found around the sunlit edges of rainforest areas or closed savannah woodland country. It grows as far south as Victoria. The strong woody vine can climb to the top of forest trees or be found scrambling through woody undergrowth. The shiny leaves are rich green and often produce a thick curtain of lush foliage hanging from the canopy. From February to May, bunches of purple grapes, similar to domestic grapes, grow on the vine.

USES These grapes can be eaten raw and initially have a rather pleasant sweetish taste. This taste is shortly followed by a harsh burning sensation in the throat. Three or four of these grapes are usually enough for most people.

NATIVE MONSTERA
Rhaphidophora pinnata

A CLIMBING VINE OF TROPICAL rainforest regions, very similar in appearance to the cultivated Monstera that is often used as an indoor plant (and is often called monsterio). The broad split-leafed vine climbs to the forest canopy in search of sunlight, where the elongated fruit are produced throughout the year. The fruit are rarely seen from ground level. Fully grown fruit take months to ripen in a darkened place. Fruit gradually ripens from the base to the apex.

USES The soft pink flesh has a spicy fruit-salad like taste. Care should be taken to avoid the jointed skin of the fruit, and the spiky black hairs lodged in these joints.

OENPELLI GRAPE
Cayratia maritima

THIS GRAPE IS FOUND IN COASTAL northern Queensland and the Northern Territory, around the fringes of flood plains, swamps and black soil areas that are inundated during the wet season, usually on low-lying coastal plains. This distinctive climbing vine scrambles over shrubs or grows up into the canopy of trees. The 'trunk' can become quite robust and the foliage consists of leathery green leaves with bluntly serrated edges, in groups of three. From the wet season to the middle of the year, bunches of purple–black grapes are produced. They can be up to 2 cm across, slightly flattened on the ends, and contain a single stone or seed.

USES The grapes are edible raw and have a sweet taste, with a slight harshness on the throat afterwards.

OTHER NAMES Native grape

THE PADDYMELON IS POISONOUS. Even though it looks and smells edible, it is not. It is a vine-like plant, which produces various-sized but often quite large round melons. It appears immediately following rainfall and in some outback areas the sides of roads are lined with thousands of these melons. Inside, the seeds are yellow and the pulp extremely bitter.

USES In some regions the juice from the melon was used as a bush medicine. The melons were heated and the warm juice rubbed onto skin infections such as ringworm and scabies.

OTHER NAMES Camel melon

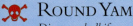

ROUND YAM
Dioscorea bulbifera

THIS YAM IS POISONOUS UNLESS prepared properly. The yam vine is common in monsoon forests and open forests in the North and favours sandy loamy soil. It appears after the wet season, from February to May. The vine, with its large heart-shaped leaves, climbs and scrambles over other trees and low bushes. The plant has tiny flowers. The underground yam grows to about the size of a large onion. It is dirty brown in colour and has a hairy appearance.

USES Aboriginal people would only eat this yam after extensive preparation. This would include baking or boiling the yam, removing the skin, grating or pounding the yellowish flesh, washing the pulp in water for at least 10 hours, and then baking it again. After all that, the final taste is pretty similar to boiled potatoes.

OTHER NAMES Cheeky yam

SUPPLE JACK
Flagellaria indica

SUPPLE JACK IS REASONABLY widespread in northern Australia and can be found around rainforest fringes or disturbed areas. It also favours the scrub around creek lines. The vine is present throughout the year. A distinctive climbing cane-like vine, supple jack has unusual grass-like leaves with tendrils extending from the tip, to curl around tree branches and assist with climbing. At various times of the year, tiny cream-coloured flower heads or clusters of small berries are present on the ends of the canes.

USES The very young leafy shoots and terminal buds of the vine were used as a food source. These can be eaten raw or cooked, and although rather stringy have a taste similar to spinach or cabbage. The berries and the flowers are edible. Young shoots were crushed and mixed with water, and the mixture drunk to relieve toothache, sore throat or chest complaints. The stems were also used in weaving and baskets.

WILD CUCUMBER
Cucumis sp.

THE NATIVE MELON IS A SCRAMBLING vine found in closed tropical savannah and open woodland country. The main stem is rough to touch. The bell-shaped flowers are small and bright orange–yellow. The small melon-like fruit is in season from March to May. They are smooth-skinned, oval and covered in fine hairs. Inside, the fruit resembles a cucumber.

USES The edible fruit tastes a little like a sweet cucumber. The fruit is eaten when it is white to yellow in colour and has fallen off the vine.

OTHER NAMES Bush cucumber

THESE WILD GRAPES ARE FOUND IN closed tropical woodland and open woodland, often beside waterways. The grapes are produced on a climbing vine, which tends to scramble over other vegetation, particularly trees. The leaves have serrated edges and are grouped in a trifoliate structure. Opposite each leaf structure there is a climbing tendril. From February to April bunches of grape-like fruit are produced. These bunches have been recorded up to 1 kg in weight. Initially the fruit is round and green in colour. Mature grapes are dark purple and flattish in shape. Each grape has one small seed.

USES The grapes can be eaten raw. They have a sweet but slightly acidic taste and are harsh on the throat. The underground roots can also be eaten after roasting. The juice of the vine was used by Aboriginal people as a reputed cure for death adder bites. Early settlers ate these, along with other grapes, and sometimes made them into jam.

OTHER NAMES Native grapes

WILD INDIGO
Tephrosea purpurea

WILD INDIGO IS COMMON BEHIND sand dunes along the northern coastline, but also grows in well-drained sandy soil along creek lines and riverbanks. The plant, which resembles a weed, grows to about 60 cm. It produces a flower head of small purple pea-like flowers and miniature pea pods. The foliage consists of a main stem with opposite leaflets all the way along in a herringbone fashion. Indigo can be found all year round, but is most prevalent during the wet season or after rain.

USES The plant was used as a fish poison. The entire plant, particularly the root system, was crushed up and washed in small rocky catchments of water to poison fish. Within a few minutes, the stupefied fish rise to the surface, where they were easily caught. The fish could then be cooked in the usual way.

MAGPIE GOOSE (EGGS)
Anseranas semipalmata

MAGPIE GEESE, OR PIED GEESE, inhabit swamps and wetlands and are abundant in northern Australia. These large black and white birds congregate in flocks of several hundred or more and are often seen and heard honking their way across the sky at last light. Their eggs are generally found in abundance toward the latter part of the wet season, February – April. At this time the water in the swamplands is deep enough to support their floating nests, which are most often constructed from masses of **spikerush** (*Eleocharis dulcis*). These floating nests, all but impossible to sight from the edge of the swamp, are about one metre in diameter and may contain up to 16 eggs. One traditional method for hunting goose eggs was to go out in the waters in bark canoes.

USES The cream-coloured eggs are about three times the size of domestic duck eggs and have a very similar taste when cooked. They have a high nutritional value and were prized as a delicacy.

OTHER NAMES Pied goose eggs

BARRAMUNDI
Lates calcarifer

THE BARRAMUNDI COMMONLY inhabits inshore waters and estuaries, and can be found quite a distance up tropical rivers into freshwater bill-abongs and waterholes. A large silver fish with metallic green or bronze back, it can grow to over a metre in length. The 'barra' shelters around rocks, snags and weed beds during the day, then starts feeding in the late afternoon. Barra hunt at night in fresh waters and the loud 'chop' of night-feeding barra is a good indication of their presence. The fish can be speared during the day or at night by torchlight, when they often enter the shallows and reflect a brilliant red-eye shine. Line fishing is most successful in the evening or early morning. When handling the fish be careful of the sharp, serrated gill covers, which can cut to the bone.

USES Traditionally cooked on hot coals or sometimes wrapped in leaves or paperbark. The fish can be filleted and grilled, or cooked whole.

OTHER NAMES Barra, giant perch

BLACK BREAM
Hephaestus spp., *Scortum* spp.

A FRESHWATER FISH INHABITING dams and billabongs through to sluggish inland rivers and fast-flowing rainforest streams. It can grow to over 5 kg in weight but is more often caught around 1–2 kg. Colour ranges from a light khaki to almost black, often with a greenish tinge, and sometimes with orange to yellow patches. After death, it turns jet black within a few minutes. Suitable line baits can vary from red meat, freshwater prawns, mussels or worms to fruit, such as the **cluster fig** (*Ficus racemosa*). A small to medium-sized hook is best, fished on the bottom around snags, rocks and weed beds, or at the bottom of waterfalls or rapids. Fin spines and spikes on either side of the gills are very sharp.

USES Aboriginal people would traditionally spear the bream using a spear with multiple, thin, sharp prongs. It is best cooked whole in the ashes, or wrapped in wet paperbark or leaves and roasted in hot coals for about 20 minutes.

OTHER NAMES Sooty grunter

CATFISH, FORK-TAILED
Arius leptaspis

THIS FISH INHABITS TROPICAL inshore waters and estuaries, and the freshwater reaches of larger river systems. It can grow to well over 10 kg and has six fleshy 'whiskers' around the mouth and a smooth, slimy skin, often with a metallic sheen. The catfish is easily line-caught on baits of fish-flesh, red meat, or just about anything resembling food. They are best fished for on the bottom, where they use their sensory whiskers to locate food. Spearing is difficult due to the tough bony plate over the head and front of the body. The three main fins carry stout sharp spines that can inflict serious injury. Fish should be stunned by sharp blows to the head with a blunt instrument, and the spines removed with pliers as soon as the fish is caught.

USES Roasted whole on hot coals, wrapped in leaves or wet paperbark, or filleted and skinned prior to grilling. Larger specimens can be coarse and fatty, but young fish are surprisingly tasty.

OTHER NAMES Croaker, salmon catfish

FISH

STINGRAYS ARE WIDELY DISTRIBUTED and occur in estuaries, bays and coral reef flats, sometimes penetrating the freshwater reaches of rivers. They are usually bottom dwellers and often enter quite shallow water due to their flattened profile. Large numbers of stingrays often swarm over sand flats and shallow reefs with the rising tide. The stingray has a broad, flattened disk-shaped body, and a long whip-like tail. It can grow to 2 m across the flaps. The eyes are on the upper surface; the mouth and gills are underneath.

USES Aboriginal people would usually spear stingrays. Great care is needed in handling them as the tails bear one or two sharp, barbed, venomous spines. Applying warm to hot water to a wound is the best method of breaking down the venom. Stingray flaps can be roasted over hot coals or skinned and grilled. They have a tasty, fish-like flavour. The barb from the tail could be used as a knife or spear point.

GREEN ANT
Oecophylla smaragdina

THESE ANTS ARE FOUND IN OPEN woodland, closed tropical woodland and some tropical forest fringe areas. The nest consists of bunches of green leaves matted or fused together. The leaves are usually a living part of the host tree or plant and the nests are often suspended some distance above ground level. Despite their common name the ants only have a green abdomen, the rest of the body structure being yellow or orange. The ants are easily disturbed and can drop onto an unwary intruder from overhead and surrounding foliage. They inflict a number of short painful bites.

USES Aboriginal people ate the white larvae found inside the leafy nests. This has a pleasant lemon taste. The ants and larvae were also pounded and mixed with water to produce a lime-flavoured drink that was taken to relieve colds, headaches and sore throats. The concoction is mixed very thoroughly, until a milky colouring is produced.

OTHER NAMES Green tree ants

INSECT/GRUB

THESE ANTS ARE ONLY FOUND around Harts Range, north-east of Alice Springs, and Papunya, north-west of Alice. The ants construct their nest in the flat red sandy soil, under a bush or tree. The entrance is invariably camouflaged among the dead litter and foliage of the host tree. There is one entrance to the underground chambers. The 'feeder' ants collect nectar before taking it underground to give to the 'storers' who hide in the side chambers. Gradually the storers become so engorged with nectar that they swell, to about the size of a marble. The stored honey can be seen in the ants' stretched abdomens, and when food is short, can be regurgitated for the worker ants.

USES Aboriginal women would start digging about half a metre from the main entrance, working around in a circular fashion trying to locate the numerous side chambers leading off from the main channel. The honey is sucked from the ants' abdomens. It is strong, rich and intensely sweet.

OTHER NAMES Honey pot ants

LERP SCALE

Psylla eucalypti, Psylla spp., *Glycaspis* spp.

MANY SPECIES OF GUM TREES IN drier areas are host plants for the lerp scale. The actual insect is a minute pink-coloured grub, a psyllid bug, which sucks the sap of eucalyptus leaves. In this process the leaves become covered with a wafer-thin white crusty scale, and a heavy infestation gives the leaves a white, furry appearance.

USES The white scale can be removed from the gum leaves with the thumbnail and eaten. It has a pleasant, sugary, eucalyptus taste. The scale also dissolves in water, and was used to make a drink. Look for it in the dry season – you won't see it after rain as it is washed off the leaves.

OTHER NAMES Manna

NATIVE BEE (SUGARBAG)
Trigona spp.

THE TOTAL DISTRIBUTION OF THE native bee is not known. The map shows the spread of the bees' favoured trees (e.g. *Eucalyptus terminalis, E. microtheca* and *Xanthorrhoea* spp.) but it is most likely that the bees' distribution exceeds this. Native bees appear to be particularly common in The Kimberley. Native bee hives, or 'sugarbag', are notoriously difficult to find. Usually they are located in the hollow branches and trunks of trees. The entrance is a small aperture ringed by a dark brown waxy ridge or lining. The bees, which have no sting, are smaller than a housefly. Aboriginals would sometimes follow the bee's flight path by attaching a piece of down to the abdomen or sprinkling fine white dust or chalk over the bee. Once the tree is located, the hive's position would be detected by placing an ear against the trunk for signs of internal activity.

USES Sugarbag is one of the most prized of all bush tuckers. It provides energy but is also delicious. The honey is scooped out, with the larvae and bees, and eaten. It is never cooked or used with other foods.

WITCHETTY GRUB
Cossidae sp.

THE WITCHETTY GRUB IS PROBABLY one of the best known sources of bush food in Australia. The grub is the larva of a moth. In the drier regions of Australia these grubs are regularly found in the root system of the **witchetty bush** (*Acacia kempeana*). However, they are also to be found in eucalyptus species, particularly **bloodwoods** (*Eucalyptus terminalis*). The grubs are white in colour with a hard head. When fully grown they are about the size of a man's thumb. The grubs can be found all year though not every witchetty bush yields these tasty morsels.

USES The entire grub, including the head, can be eaten raw and has a very pleasant buttery taste. They can also be lightly cooked on hot coals or pan fried. When cooked, they have a taste similar to scrambled eggs. The grubs contain valuable protein and fats.

Freshwater Turtle
Chelodina rugosa

Small freshwater turtles can be found in swamps, lagoons, billabongs and waterways in general. The upper shell is mud-coloured and the lower shell is white or cream. In swamp areas, the turtles move among the grass and reeds attached to the muddy bottom, which provide camouflage and protection. To catch the turtles, Aboriginal women would wade into the water, 'feeling' with their feet, or poking in the mud with a stick to detect the smooth, hard shell of the turtle. The turtle could also be caught using a fishing line and fresh meat.

USES The turtle was traditionally cooked in an earth oven or placed directly upside down on hot coals. The majority of white meat is in and around the leg joints, under the body plate. This plate is easily removed once the turtle has been completely cooked. The meat is oily with a strong chicken-like flavour.

OTHER NAMES Snake neck turtle

GOULDS GOANNA
Varanus gouldii

A LARGE GOANNA, GROWING TO 1.6 m in length, that is found throughout most of the mainland of Australia. Colour varies depending on location, and ranges from light yellow to almost black, with numerous scattered lighter and darker flecks forming irregular cross-bands. The flattened, keeled tail has a white or pale-yellow tip. This goanna lives in burrows or hollow logs. The tail leaves a snake-like track, with claw-prints either side, so hunters could track the goanna to its lair. These goannas have very sharp claws and can inflict a painful bite.

USES These goannas were – and still are in some regions – an important bush tucker. The goanna would be cooked whole on the ashes or over hot coals. The oily white meat has a flavour similar to chicken. The intestines would be searched for eggs, as such a nutritious food would never be ignored.

OTHER NAMES Goulds sand goanna, sand monitor

HAWKSBILL TURTLE (EGGS)
Eretmochelys imbricata

LARGE HAWKSBILL TURTLES CAN BE found in Australia's northern coastal waters. The turtles lay their eggs principally at night. The female turtle crawls up the beach to a sandy area above the high tide mark to select the nesting site. There she digs a hole over a metre in diameter and up to three-quarters of a metre deep. Up to 100 round, white eggs are deposited into the hole by the female. They are then covered with sand and the turtle returns to the sea. The female leaves two track signs on the beach sand – one from the water to the nesting site, and the other from the nesting site to the water. Aboriginal people would follow these tracks when hunting for eggs. Feral pigs are quick to detect newly laid eggs and root them up. The slightest movement of the eggs kills the embryo inside the shell. Stay well away from the turtles and the nests.

USES Turtle eggs were valued for their rich flavour and nutritional value. Aboriginal people would sometimes eat the eggs raw whilst out hunting.

NOTE Turtles are a protected species.

SCRUB PYTHON
Morelia amethystina

THE SCRUB PYTHON INHABITS tropical rainforest areas on the east coast of Queensland. It is Australia's largest python. This python has an unpredictable temperament and can inflict a severe but not toxic bite. This python usually moves around at night seeking prey – mice, bush rats and even small wallabies. During the day, it can often be found in sunlit areas, such as along track systems, on warm rocks and logs.

USES The scrub python was traditionally cooked on an open fire for about one hour. Firstly the skin was lightly singed over the fire and the scales scraped off using a knife. The snake was then tightly coiled and placed on the hot coals. The coiled bands of the snake were held together by skewering, using splintered pieces of wood. The coiled snake was turned over every 10 minutes or so to ensure even cooking. The entrails were removed and discarded. The thick white flesh, which resembles chicken in both appearance and texture, was then eaten.

WATER PYTHONS ARE OFTEN FOUND in hollow logs or crevices around waterways, swamps and lagoons. Unless disturbed, they are generally nocturnal. This python is not an aggressive snake and usually bites only when provoked. The snake has a yellow- or apricot-coloured belly and shiny brown back scales. The average length is 2–3 m.

USES Aboriginal people in northern Australia still regard the water python as a great food source. The skin of the snake is singed over an open fire and the burnt scales scraped from the body. The snake is then coiled, the various coils being fastened together using wooden skewers. The coiled snake is placed on the hot coals and allowed to cook for about an hour. After cooking, the intestines are removed and carefully searched for eggs. These eggs taste very similar to boiled domestic eggs. The white flesh of the snake has a taste similar to chicken meat.

BLACK LIP OYSTER
Saccostrea echinata

BLACK LIP OYSTERS ARE RESTRICTED to northern coastal waters. The large, round or elongated shells of these oysters are found attached to rocky surfaces. The rough shell has a hinge area at one end. Inside, the black lip oyster is quite large and attractive, with a smooth white shell and black fringe around the edge.

USES The complete oyster shell can be dislodged from the rock with a sharp tap, using a metal instrument, or another rock as a hammer. Open the shell by piercing the hinge with a sharp, strong metal instrument (e.g. strong knife). Do not attempt to prise open the shell using bare hands, as this invariably results in lacerations. Cuts from the shells' sharp edges are often slow to heal. Aboriginal people would roast the complete oyster shell quickly over a hot fire. The heat of the fire causes the shell to open. The oysters have quite a strong taste, and a high iodine content.

CHITON
Chiton spp.

THIS SHELLFISH CAN BE FOUND clinging to rocks in coastal areas across northern Australia. The best place to look for them is between high and low tide levels, but their camouflage and preference for crevices can make them difficult to find. A series of plates across the back of the mollusc give it the appearance of an armadillo. A tough, roughened skirt surrounds the plated shell to further protect the animal. The creature often curls up into a ball when removed from the rocks. A sharp blow, or prising with a stout object, is often required to break its suction on hard surfaces.

USES Traditionally, Aboriginal people would roast the shellfish on hot coals for about five minutes. They can also be boiled for around 10 minutes. Either way, the flesh is tough and leathery, like a chewy piece of ham with a prawn-like flavour.

SHELLFISH

COCKLE SHELL
Anadora granosa

COCKLE SHELLS, FOUND AROUND the coast in northern Australia, look like miniature clam shells. The two halves are identical, with raised ribs radiating from the hinge area to the scalloped edge. These shellfish were extremely popular with Aboriginal people, and even today vast shell middens can be found around the coastline of northern Australia. These middens, or mounds of old shells, represent what was once an Aboriginal refuse or garbage dump. Some of them date back hundreds, or possibly thousands, of years. The shells can be gathered easily during low tide around rocky headlands and shallow coastal reef areas. They are invariably found in the water at shallow depth. In some areas they are still an important part of the traditional Aboriginal diet.

USES The shells were usually roasted on hot coals or boiled before being eaten. The edible flesh tastes similar to an oyster.

FRESHWATER MUSSEL
Velesunio spp.

RIVERS, STREAMS AND BILLABONGS of north and eastern Australia invariably contain some form of freshwater mussel. The animal is protected by two identical shells hinged together, generally dark brown or black on the outside, 'mother-of-pearl' on the inside. Although usually 5–10 cm long, they can sometimes be up to 20 cm. In still water, freshwater mussels may leave a 'track' through the soft sand or mud bottom, at the end of which may be found a small mound covering the shellfish. They also occur amongst waterweeds and reeds.

USES Mussels usually contain sand and grit and are best kept in a container of fresh water overnight to allow the grit to pass through the animal. Then they can be boiled for a few minutes with a little salt, during which time the shell will open to reveal the meat inside. Mussels have a strong, shellfish taste. Aboriginal people traditionally ate them raw, or roasted in hot ashes.

FRESHWATER PRAWN

Macrobrachium australiense

A VARIETY OF FRESHWATER PRAWNS are found in Australia. Those in the east coast rainforest regions are smaller than those from northern Australia generally. They are distinguished by their thin nippers or pincers and are extremely timid. Due to the clarity of the waters, they can often detect movement on the bank. They are particularly attracted by meat bait. At night, they can be located by their red eye-shine that reflects torch light. They can sometimes be caught by hand. The long, flexible tendrils of the **lawyer vine** (*Calamus* spp.), were used by Aboriginal people to jag the freshwater prawns. The tapered end of the tendrils, with its hooked thorns, was slowly moved in front of the inquisitive prawn. When the prawn tried to eat the tendril or bait, the tendril would be given a sharp thrust and pulled in. The prawn, impaled on the recurved thorns, was caught.

USES These crustaceans are still a popular bush tucker. They taste quite like an ordinary prawn.

OTHER NAMES Yabby

MANGROVE SNAIL
Nerita spp.

THE MANGROVE SNAIL IS FOUND along Australia's northern coast. It can be found throughout the year, often clinging to rocks at low tide, although it is more prolific in mangrove areas, where it attaches itself to the prop-roots of mangrove trees above the waterline. It has a snail-like shell, which is often deeply ribbed, and can be grey, brown or black in colour.

USES Shellfish were, and still are, an important source of food along the northern coastal areas. The snails are boiled for about 10 minutes, but can also be roasted on hot coals. The shells are broken open with a rock, and the gristly flesh is eaten after removing the 'trap door' that adheres to the muscle. *Nerita* have a salty, shellfish-like taste, and are rather tough and chewy. They also make excellent bait for line-fishing around mangrove areas.

OTHER NAMES Black nerites

MANGROVE WORM
Teredo sp.

THE TEREDO WORM IS FOUND IN the rotting wood and logs of mangrove swamps in northern Australia. It looks like a worm but is actually a mollusc. The worm is grey in colour, up to 45 cm in length and extremely soft and pliable, except for the hard wood-chewing head.

USES Aboriginal people eat the mangrove worm in small quantities, as a tonic for general sickness. It is available throughout the year and was usually sought during periods of low tide. The body of the worm is eaten raw and tastes similar to oysters. The hard head was not eaten.

MUD CRAB
Scylla serrata

SHELLFISH

MANGROVE-LINED SHORES AND muddy estuaries are the home of the mud crab, which lives in burrows or holes. The body is usually greenish brown, sometimes with a bluish tinge. Large examples can measure 25 cm across the shell and weigh over 2 kg. The claws are very heavy and powerful, making the mud crab a dangerous animal to handle. Aboriginal people sometimes use a long stick with a short hooked end to 'hook' the crabs from their burrows. Mud crabs often leave circular, shallow depressions across the mud flats. When the women are out hunting they might prod with a stick at low tide to find the occasional crab buried in the mud.

USES Mud crabs are an excellent – and delicious – tucker, still highly prized in northern Australia. They are traditionally roasted on hot coals, but can also be thrown into boiling water and simmered for 10 to 20 minutes. As they cook, the colour changes to orange. Live crabs are best killed immediately, although crab meat turns bad quickly and must be cooked straight away.

MUD MUSSEL

Polymesoda coaxans

MUD MUSSELS ARE LARGE SHELLFISH found embedded in the mud flats of mangrove areas, usually between the mangroves and dry land. Sometimes there will be the scattered remains of old dry shells: these black or brown shells often have a silver 'hinge' area, where the two halves were once joined. On the outside of all mud mussel shells, faint radiating lines are engraved on the casings. The mussels move around the softer mud areas. One technique for locating them was to walk or feel in the mud using the feet or hands. During drier periods, the mussels become trapped in the caked mud and are often embedded deep inside the cracks. A small portion of the shell is visible in the base of the mud crack.

USES Mussels were usually cooked in their shells on a fire, or alternatively, cracked open and the extracted mussel boiled in water. They have a distinctive seafood taste and are quite palatable.

OTHER NAMES Mud oysters

MUD WHELKS ARE FOUND ON THE mangrove mud, just below the high-tide mark throughout the year. The shell is a distinctive spiral shape and resembles a small ice-cream cone. When disturbed, the animal retreats inside the shell to reveal a purple-coloured inner shell-lining.

USES To eat the animal inside the shell, the shell is roasted on hot coals for about five minutes. Then the shell is broken open by striking it with a rock at the opening or base end of the shell. Another method is to poke the shells, point-first, into hot ashes and wait for the animal to be steamed in its own juices. It then comes partly out of the shell and can be removed without having to crack the shell. The cooked flesh has a pleasant, mussel-like taste.

MUD WHELK
Terebralia sp.

THE MUD WHELK SHELL IS A distinctive spiral shape and resembles a small ice-cream cone. The shells are found on the mangrove mud, around the high tide mark, throughout the year. When disturbed, the animal retreats inside the shell to reveal a purple-coloured inner shell-lining.

USES To cook the animal, the shells should be boiled for around 10 minutes, or roasted on hot coals for about 5 minutes. Break the shell open by striking it with a rock at the opening or base end of the shell. The cooked animal can be removed from the shell and eaten after discarding the thumbnail-like trapdoor. In taste it is similiar to a mussel.

 THE COLOURFUL PAINTED CRAY CAN be found around northern coastal waters. They are similar to other crayfish except for their vividly coloured shell. Unlike many other crayfish, it is almost impossible to catch them in a trap or pot. The best method is to dive underwater with a hand spear and catch them as they hide under the coral overhangs and in crevices. They can also be caught at night, using a torch, in small rock pools around exposed reefs, at low tide. When handling a live crayfish, a tough leather or rubber glove should be worn. Once held in the hand, the crays flick their tails violently trying to escape. They also emit a piercing creaking noise, from the base joint of their feelers. The sound travels through water and is an immediate signal to any nearby sharks. For this reason, the crayfish should be removed from the water as quickly as possible.

USES Crayfish can be cooked by boiling in water, or cooked over hot coals, for about 10 minutes.

OTHER NAMES Coral crayfish

ROCK OYSTER
Saccostrea spp.

AROUND NORTHERN COASTAL AREAS, large clusters of rock oysters are often found adhering to rocky surfaces between the high- and low-water marks. They sometimes form a 'shelf' protruding from ocean-washed vertical rock faces. The oyster is usually up to 5 cm long, and consists of two shells with the upper shell like a hinged lid. The shellfish inside is plump and white.

USES The oysters can be eaten raw or cooked. The shell can be opened by piercing the hinge with a sharp strong object and then levering the lid off to reveal the mollusc. Aboriginal people would collect clusters of oysters from the rocks, then roast them quickly over a fire. The heat causes the individual shells to open. Care should be taken to avoid being cut by the sharp edges of the shells as infection usually follows. Do not attempt to prise open the oyster shell using bare hands as this invariably results in lacerations.

YABBY
Cherax spp.

THE COMMON FRESHWATER YABBY is distributed throughout all Australian mainland states. It is found in inland lagoons, billabongs, waterways and dams. These yabbies grow to a considerable size. Although present throughout the year, they tend to hibernate in mud burrows from June to August. In captive water sources such as lagoons, billabongs and dams, their population density can reach as much as 20 per square metre. The yabby is most often caught by dangling a piece of red meat on a string into the water. The yabby begins to feed on the meat, which is gently pulled to the surface. Once the yabby's long thin 'whiskers' break the water surface, it should be quickly scooped out onto the bank. They can also be enticed into traps and speared by hand.

USES Yabbies make excellent eating. They should be boiled, preferably in salt water, for about 8 minutes, and the white meat of the tail section eaten.

OTHER NAMES Freshwater yabby, Western crayfish

INDEX

Commelina sp. (scurvy weed) 4

conkerberry (konkleberry, bush plum) (*Carissa lanceolata*) 30

convolvulus (goats foot, morning glory) (*Ipomoea pes-caprae*) 129

coolibah (river ghost gum) (*Eucalyptus microtheca*) 68

coral crayfish (painted crayfish) (*Panulirus ornatus*) 173

coral tree (batwing coral tree, cork tree) (*Erythrina vespertilio*) 53

cork tree (batwing coral tree, coral tree) (*Erythrina vespertilio*) 53

corkwood tree (hakea) (*Hakea* spp.) 69

Cossidae sp. (witchetty grub) 156

cotton tree (yellow hibiscus, beach hibiscus) (*Hibiscus tiliaceus*) 70

crabs eye (gidgee gidgee, rosary pea) (*Abrus precatorius*) 128

creek fig (sandpaper fig, purple fig) (*Ficus coronata*) 105

creeping hibiscus (climbing hibiscus, bush carrot) (*Abelmoschus moschatus*) 125

creeping saltbush (ruby saltbush) (*Enchylaena tomentosa*) 45

croaker (fork-tailed catfish, salmon catfish) (*Arius leptaspis*) 150

Cucumis sp. (wild cucumber, bush cucumber) 144

cunjevoi (spoon lily) (*Alocasia macrorrhizos*) 31

Cyathea spp. (tree fern) 112

cycad (*Cycas* spp.) 23

Cycas spp. (cycad) 23

Cymbidium canaliculatum (tree orchid, rock orchid, black orchid) 27

Cystococcus sp. (bloodwood apple, bloodwood gall, insect gall, bush coconut, bush apple) 26

Dasyatis spp. (*Himantura* spp.) (stingray) 151

Davidson plum (sour plum) (*Davidsonia pruriens*) 71

Davidsonia pruriens (Davidson plum, sour plum) 71

Dendrocnide excelsa (giant stinging tree, stinger, gympie gympie) 35

desert bloodwood (bloodwood) (*Eucalyptus terminalis*) 56

desert fig (native rock fig, wild fig) (*Ficus platypoda*) 42

desert oak (desert she-oak) (*Allocasuarina decaisneana*) 72

desert she-oak (desert oak) (*Allocasuarina decaisneana*) 72

desert yam (bush potato) (*Ipomoea costata*) 126

devil's guts (dodder laurel, devil's twine) (*Cassytha filiformis*) 127

devil's twine (devil's guts, dodder laurel) (*Cassytha filiformis*) 127

Dioscorea bulbifera (round yam, cheeky yam) 142

Dioscorea transversa (long yam, pencil yam) 134

dodder laurel (devil's guts, devil's twine) (*Cassytha filiformis*) 127

dog's balls (emu berry, turkey bush, dysentery bush) (*Grewia retusifolia*) 32

Duboisia hopwoodii (emu poison bush, pituri bush) 33

dugulla (black plum) (*Planchonella chartacea*) 73

dysentery bush (emu berry, turkey bush, dog's balls) (*Grewia retusifolia*) 32

Elaeocarpus bancroftii (Johnson River almond, Queensland almond) 86

Elaeocarpus grandis (blue quandong, silver quandong) 57

Eleocharis dulcis (spikerush, water chestnut) 5

Emila sonchifolia (thistle) 18

emu apple tree (*Owenia vernicosa*) 74

emu berry (turkey bush, dog's balls, dysentery bush) (*Grewia retusifolia*) 32

emu poison bush (pituri bush) (*Duboisia hopwoodii*) 33

Enchylaena tomentosa (ruby saltbush, creeping saltbush) 45

Entada phaseoloides (matchbox bean, Queensland bean) 136

Eretmochelys imbricata (hawksbill turtle – eggs) 159

Eriosema chinense (bush carrot, bush potato) 15

Erythrina vespertilio (batwing coral tree, cork tree, coral tree) 53

Eucalyptus microtheca (coolibah, river ghost gum) 68

Eucalyptus terminalis (bloodwood, desert bloodwood) 56

Eupomatia laurina (bush guava, native guava, bolwarra) 62

fan palm (*Livistona inermis*) 24

fern-leafed grevillea (golden grevillea, golden parrot tree, swamp grevillea) (*Grevillea pteridifolia*) 79

Ficus coronata (sandpaper fig, purple fig, creek fig) 105

Ficus leptoclada (apricot fig) 52

Ficus opposita (sandpaper fig, sweet, sweet sandpaper fig) 46

Ficus platypoda (native rock fig, desert fig, wild fig) 42

Ficus racemosa (cluster fig) 66

finger bean (gulaka, wild mung bean) (*Vigna radiata*) 130

fish poison tree (soap wattle) (*Acacia holosericea*) 75

Flagellaria indica (supple jack) 143

Kalumburu yam (bush potato) (*Ipomoea* sp.) 132
kapok tree (silk cotton tree, bombax, canoe tree) (*Bombax ceiba*) 107
konkleberry (bush plum, conkerberry) (*Carissa lanceolata*) 30
kurrajong (red kurrajong) (*Brachychiton paradoxum*) 89

lady apple (native apple, red bush apple) (*Syzygium suborbiculare*) 90
Lates calcarifer (barramundi, barra, giant perch) 148
lawyer vine (wait-a-while) (*Calamus* spp.) 133
Leichhardt pine (Leichhardt tree) (*Nauclea orientalis*) 91
Leichhardt tree (Leichhardt pine) (*Nauclea orientalis*) 91
lerp scale (manna) (*Psylla eucalypti*, *Psylla* spp., *Glycaspis* spp.) 154
Liasis fuscus (water python) 161
Licuala ramsayi (Cairns fan palm) 21
little gooseberry tree (green plum) (*Buchanania arborescens*) 92
Livistona inermis (fan palm) 24
Livistona spp. (cabbage tree palm) 20
lolly bush (*Clerodendrum floribundum*) 37
long yam (pencil yam) (*Dioscorea transversa*) 134
lotus lily (sacred lotus, pink waterlily, red lily) (*Nelumbo nucifera*) 1
love-in-the-mist (bush passionfruit, stinking passionfruit, wild passionfruit) (*Passiflora foetida*) 121

Macrobrachium australiense (freshwater prawn, yabby) 166
magpie goose (eggs) (pied goose eggs) (*Anseranas semipalmata*) 147
maloga bean (yellow-flowering bean, pencil yam) (*Vigna lanceolata*) 135
Mangifera indica (mango) 93
mango (*Mangifera indica*) 93
mangrove fern (*Acrostichum* sp.) 38
mangrove palm (nypa palm) (*Nypa fruticans*) 3
mangrove snail (black nerites) (*Nerita* spp.) 167
mangrove worm (*Teredo* sp.) 168
Manilkara kauki (wongi plum) 118
manna (lerp scale) (*Psylla eucalypti*, *Psylla* spp., *Glycaspis* spp.) 154
Marsdenia australis (bush banana, native pear) 120
Marsilea drummondii (nardoo, clover fern) 2
matchbox bean (Queensland bean) (*Entada phaseoloides*) 136
melaleuca (paperbark tree, tea-tree) (*Melaleuca leucadendra*) 101
Melaleuca leucadendra (paperbark tree, tea-tree, melaleuca) 101

Melophorus sp. (honey ant, honey pot ant) 153
milk bush (caustic vine, caustic bush, snake vine) (*Sarcostemma* spp.) 124
milky plum (geebung) (*Persoonia falcata*) 77
mistletoe (*Amyema* spp.) 39
monkey nut tree (peanut tree) (*Sterculia quadrifida*) 102
Morelia amethystina (scrub python) 160
Moreton Bay chestnut (blackbean) (*Castanospermum australe*) 55
Morinda citrifolia (cheese fruit, great morinda) 36
morning glory (goats foot, convolvulus) (*Ipomoea pes-caprae*) 129
mud crab (*Scylla serrata*) 169
mud mussel (mud oyster) (*Polymesoda coaxans*) 170
mud oyster (mud mussel) (*Polymesoda coaxans*) 170
mud whelk (*Telescopium telescopium*) 171
mud whelk (*Terebralia* sp.) 172
Musa acuminata (bush banana, native banana) 61
Myristica insipida (nutmeg, native nutmeg) 97

nardoo (clover fern) (*Marsilea drummondii*) 2
native apple (bush apple) (*Syzygium eucalyptoides*) 94
native apple (lady apple, red bush apple) (*Syzygium suborbiculare*) 90
native banana (bush banana) (*Musa acuminata*) 61
native bee (sugarbag) (*Trigona* spp.) 155
native caper (wild orange) (*Capparis canescens*) 116
native citrus (bush raisin, native currant) (*Psydrax latifolia*) 29
native currant (bush raisin, native citrus) (*Psydrax latifolia*) 29
native ginger (wild ginger) (*Alpinia caerulea*) 47
native gooseberry (cape gooseberry) (*Physalis peruviana*) 123
native gooseberry (*Physalis minima*) 40
native grape (*Cissus hypoglauca*) 138
native grape (Oenpelli grape) (*Cayratia maritima*) 140
native grape (wild grape) (*Ampelocissus acetosa*) 137
native grape (wild grape) (*Cayratia trifolia*) 145
native guava (bush guava, bolwarra) (*Eupomatia laurina*) 62
native hibiscus (native rosella) (*Hibiscus sabdariffa*) 43

red bush apple (lady apple, native apple) (*Syzygium suborbiculare*) 90

red kurrajong (kurrajong) (*Brachychiton paradoxum*) 89

red lily (lotus lily, sacred lotus, pink waterlily) (*Nelumbo nucifera*) 1

red-flowered saw-sedge (saw-sedge) (*Gahnia aspera*) 11

Rhaphidophora pinnata (native monstera) 139

river ghost gum (coolibah) (*Eucalyptus microtheca*) 68

river mangrove (freshwater mangrove, itchy tree) (*Barringtonia acutangula*) 76

rock orchid (tree orchid, black orchid) (*Cymbidium canaliculatum*) 27

rock oyster (*Saccostrea* spp.) 174

rosary pea (gidgee gidgee, crabs eye) (*Abrus precatorius*) 128

roseleaf raspberry (wild raspberry, rainforest raspberry, forest bramble) (*Rubus rosifolius*) 49

round yam (cheeky yam) (*Dioscorea bulbifera*) 142

Rubus rosifolius (wild raspberry, rainforest raspberry, roseleaf raspberry, forest bramble) 49

ruby saltbush (creeping saltbush) (*Enchylaena tomentosa*) 45

Saccostrea echinata (black lip oyster) 162

Saccostrea spp. (rock oyster) 174

sacred lotus (lotus lily, pink waterlily, red lily) (*Nelumbo nucifera*) 1

salmon catfish (fork-tailed catfish, croaker) (*Arius leptaspis*) 150

salty plum (gobin) (*Terminalia latipes*) 78

salty plum (Kakadu plum, billy goat plum) (*Terminalia ferdinandiana*) 87

sand monitor (Goulds goanna, Goulds sand goanna) (*Varanus gouldii*) 158

sandpaper fig (purple fig, creek fig) (*Ficus coronata*) 105

sandpaper fig, sweet (sweet sandpaper fig) (*Ficus opposita*) 46

Santalum lanceolatum (quandong, wild plum, bush plum) 104

Sarcostemma spp. (caustic vine, caustic bush, milk bush, snake vine) 124

saw-sedge (red-flowered saw-sedge) (*Gahnia aspera*) 11

Scortum spp. (*Hephaestus* spp.) (black bream, sooty grunter) 149

screw pine (pandanus) (*Pandanus* spp.) 100

scrub python (*Morelia amethystina*) 160

scurvy weed (*Commelina* sp.) 4

Scylla serrata (mud crab) 169

sea almond (tropical almond, Indian almond) (*Terminalia catappa*) 113

shampoo tree (soap tree) (*Alphitonia excelsa*) 108

she-oak (coast she-oak, whistling tree) (*Casuarina equisetifolia*) 106

silk cotton tree (bombax, kapok tree, canoe tree) (*Bombax ceiba*) 107

silver quandong (blue quandong) (*Elaeocarpus grandis*) 57

Siphonodon pendulus (tennis ball fruit) 111

snake neck turtle (freshwater turtle) (*Chelodina rugosa*) 157

snake vine (caustic vine, caustic bush, milk bush) (*Sarcostemma* spp.) 124

soap tree (shampoo tree) (*Alphitonia excelsa*) 108

soap wattle (fish poison tree) (*Acacia holosericea*) 75

Solanum echinatum (wild tomato) 50

solitaire palm (*Ptychosperma elegans*) 25

sooty grunter (black bream) (*Hephaestus* spp., *Scortum* spp.) 149

sour plum (Davidson plum) (*Davidsonia pruriens*) 71

spikerush (water chestnut) (*Eleocharis dulcis*) 5

spinifex (*Triodia* spp.) 12

spoon lily (cunjevoi) (*Alocasia macrorrhizos*) 31

Sterculia quadrifida (peanut tree, monkey nut tree) 102

stinger (giant stinging tree, gympie gympie) (*Dendrocnide excelsa*) 35

stingray (*Dasyatis* spp., *Himantura* spp.) 151

stinking passionfruit (bush passionfruit, love-in-the-mist, wild passionfruit) (*Passiflora foetida*) 121

strychnine tree (*Strychnos lucida*) 109

Strychnos lucida (strychnine tree) 109

sugarbag (native bee) (*Trigona* spp.) 155

supple jack (*Flagellaria indica*) 143

swamp grevillea (golden grevillea, golden parrot tree, fern-leafed grevillea) (*Grevillea pteridifolia*) 79

sweet sandpaper fig (sandpaper fig, sweet) (*Ficus opposita*) 46

Syzygium eucalyptoides (native apple, bush apple) 94

Syzygium johnsonii (Johnson satin ash) 85

Syzygium sp. (onion wood) 98

Syzygium suborbiculare (lady apple, native apple, red bush apple) 90

Tacca leontopetaloides (arrowroot, Polynesian arrowroot) 13

tamarind (*Tamarindus indica*) 110

Tamarindus indica (tamarind) 110

tea-tree (paperbark tree, melaleuca) (*Melaleuca leucadendra*) 101

183

Acknowledgements

PROJECT EDITOR AND MANAGER
Margaret Barca

COVER DESIGN
desertpony

INTERNAL DESIGN
Adrian Saunders

MANAGING EDITOR
Astrid Browne

EDITORIAL ASSISTANCE
Saskia Adams and Susan McLeish

INDEX
Fay Donlevy

TAXONOMIC CONSULTANT
Tony Orr, B.Sc. (Hons), Project Botanist, Defence
(Military Geographic Information Unit, Darwin)

GEOGRAPHY CONSULTANT
Raymond Pask

PHOTO CREDITS

Pages (i) Water lilies (*Nymphaea* spp.), Steve Strike (v) Les Hiddins,
Steve Strike/Explore Australia Publishing (vi) Apricot fig (*Ficus leptoclada*),
Gidgee gidgee (*Abrus precatorius*), Les Hiddins (viii) Honey ants
(*Melophorus* sp.), Les Hiddins (ix) Golden grevillea (*Grevillea pteridifolia*),
Steve Strike (x) Goanna on fire, Les Hiddins (xi) Nonda plums
(*Parinari nonda*), Les Hiddins

BUSH TUCKER FIELD GUIDE PHOTOS:
All photos by Les Hiddins, except for the following:
p. 13 Arrowroot (*Tacca leontopetaloides*), p. 149 Black Bream (*Hephaestus*
spp., *Scortum* spp.), p. 163 Chiton (*Chiton* spp.), p. 68 Coolibah (*Eucalyptus
microtheca*), p. 166 Freshwater prawn (*Macrobrachium australiense*), p. 10
Giant Spear Grass (*Heteropogon triticeus*), p. 83 Guava (*Psidium guajava*),
p. 41 Native Kapok Bush (*Cochlospermum fraseri*), p. 109 Strychnine Tree
(*Strychnos lucida*), p. 143 Supple Jack (*Flagellaria indica*), p. 27 Tree Orchid
(*Cymbidium canaliculatum*), p. 144 Wild Cucumber (*Cucumis* sp.), Tony Orr
p. 122 Bush Potato (*Brachystelma glabriflorum*), Paul Forster, p. 123 Cape
Gooseberry (*Physalis peruviana*), p. 105 Sandpaper Fig (*Ficus coronata*)
Glenn Leiper, p. 120 Bush Banana (*Marsdenia australis*), Steve Strike

FRONT COVER: Les Hiddins, Steve Strike/Explore Australia Publishing
Bush tucker, reading clockwise from top right:
Pandanus (*Pandanus* spp.), Ted Mead
Nonda plums (*Parinari nonda*), Les Hiddins
Bush bananas (*Marsdenia australis*), Steve Strike
Apricot figs (*Ficus leptoclada*), Les Hiddins

BACK COVER: Les Hiddins, Steve Strike/Explore Australia Publishing